Explosion of Love

Gautam Sachdeva

YogiImpressions®

YogiImpressions®
EXPLOSION OF LOVE
First published in India in 2011 by
Yogi Impressions Books Pvt. Ltd.
1711, Centre 1, World Trade Centre,
Cuffe Parade, Mumbai 400 005, India.
Website: www.yogiimpressions.com

First Edition, December 2011

ISBN 978-81-88479-86-3

Printed at: Repro India Ltd., Mumbai

Dedicated to
Ramesh S. Balsekar

"There is another world...
*but it is this one."**

* Based on a famous quote of the French poet Paul Eluard.

CONTENTS

The Ouroborus xi

Introduction xiii

Forms of the Formless 1

Lessons from the Little Teacher 32

Where You are Meant to Be 39

The Extremity of God's Will 47

Nothing Short of a Miracle! 62

Awakening from the Dream 73

The Door to Paradise 79

Nothing and the Centaur 91

The Eternal Echo 99

The End of Duality 112

Consciousness and the Fenix 129

No Greater Love 164

Acknowledgements 174

THE OUROBORUS

An ancient mythological symbol, the Ouroborus depicts a snake swallowing its own tail and in the process, forming a circle. It devours itself while at the same time regenerating itself. Both the dualities of birth and death are aspects of its existence. Through the aspect of mortality it becomes the symbol of immortality, and through the assimilation of this process it becomes a symbol of the eternal unity of all things – the symbol of One.

What is this mortality and immortality signified by the Ouroborus? Over eons, hundreds of thousands of births and deaths have taken place. Bodies have been born, bodies have died. The physical body is mortal.

In between birth and death is existence itself. Existence, which for the human being means consciousness. Right from the moment of conception till the moment of death, consciousness is the animating force in the body. You are reading this because you are conscious. I wrote it because I am conscious. Without consciousness, neither the reading nor the writing could happen, as we would be two inert bodies.

Because of Consciousness, the world *is*. Because of Consciousness, you *are*. Consciousness is Eternal. No one or nothing else needs to be venerated or worshipped for Consciousness is all there is. All else is an appearance in Consciousness, including the gods we worship. Isn't it obvious? If we were not conscious, we would not be able to worship any gods. One day a man who thought he was posing a clever question to Sri Nisargadatta Maharaj asked the sage what would he do if Lord Shiva and Lord Vishnu came and stood before him? He was flummoxed and quite offended when Maharaj told him that he would ask them to leave immediately. For he was not interested in what came because it would, sooner or later, leave. He was only interested in the Eternal – That which always *is*. Of course, Maharaj was merely trying to point out to the man that even in order to see Shiva and Vishnu, one needed to be conscious.

This is what the Ouroborus shows us: what we truly are is not the mortal body but the eternal, immortal Consciousness. Consciousness is 'you', 'me', 'he' and 'she'.

In Alchemy, the most coveted goal is the Philosopher's Stone, which is capable of transforming base metal into gold. It is also considered to be the elixir of life that confers immortality. The Ouroborus is an important symbol in Alchemy, signifying that 'the end is the beginning is the end'. The famous drawing of the Ouroborus in the Alchemical text *The Chrysopoeia of Cleopatra* depicts the snake wrapped around some words that translate as: 'One is the All'.

One, which is not the opposite of the number two; One, which simply means 'not two'; One, which is prior to all divisions yet includes all of them – this 'One' is Consciousness. 'There is another world, but it is this one.'

INTRODUCTION

One lazy Sunday morning, over a cup of *chai* (tea) at a restaurant near the Mahalakshmi temple in Mumbai, my friends and I decided to visit the *samadhi* (final resting place) of the guru of the famous sage Nisargadatta Maharaj, as it was only ten minutes away by car. Nisargadatta Maharaj was one of the leading 20th century exponents of the Indian philosophy of Advaita (non-duality). He was largely uneducated and not familiar with the scriptures, yet the world flocked to his little attic in a middle-class district of Mumbai after the publication of *I Am That – Talks with Sri Nisargadatta Maharaj* in 1973.

Maharaj was not in favour of having a samadhi for himself, as his entire teaching was based on the concept that 'you are not the body'. So, we thought we could instead visit his guru's samadhi, to pay our respects to the sage whose disciple turned out to be one of the greatest contemporary masters of Advaita to emerge from this land. Without hesitation, off we went in a cab.

As the taxi veered through a narrow street, I felt a sense of measured fear arising gradually within me. It was something like when you're walking on a lonely street late at night knowing there is no one following you, yet you keep looking over your shoulder just to make sure. There was a part of me watching the fear, and another part experiencing it. It was strange. Soon, the taxi came to a halt and we got out. I realised that my heart was beating faster for some reason I could not fathom. When we entered the courtyard, my friend Vikram asked me to sit down on the ledge to remove my shoes before stepping into the samadhi area.

That was when the chips began to fall into place. For when I raised my head to look up, my eyes fell on two iron caskets lying about forty feet away to the right, which served as funeral pyres in which the wood was placed to cremate the dead. It was only then that it dawned on me that we were at the Banganga cremation grounds. It was on that very same ledge that, twenty years ago, as a young boy, I sat with my family, watching my father's funeral pyre burn bright in the night.

Suddenly, my friend, oblivious to the feelings swarming through my heart, called out, "Look straight ahead, not to the right." As I looked, not even ten feet away, was Sri Siddharameshwar Maharaj's samadhi.

I was amazed that I had been brought back to this same spot, after a gap of twenty years, by a teaching that taught the exact opposite of what I thought when I was a boy of fourteen. I had thought that death was the end of everything – story over! *The damning physical evidence of a dead body right there staring straight into one's eyes.*

As a child, fear would arise on the numerous occasions when I would see, on the Mumbai roads, a small group of men dressed in white, carrying a bier – a body wrapped in a white shroud with flowers strewn over it. My hair would stand on end. What a finality those scenes had – death as the end of it all. The thought would arise… 'I don't want to die'. This thought would promptly be followed by the next thought: 'You may not want to, but you will die one day'. I used to wonder, 'What will happen to me when I'm dead?'

A thought, similar to that, was expressed by a friend of mine recently. She said that she could still remember the dread she would feel as a child, when she would open the newspaper and look at the obituaries. She was told that all those pictures she saw were of people who were 'dead'. The natural deduction was that one day, her photo would be on that page as well, and this would leave her very sad and confused.

In my childhood, I remember hearing a Hindi song whose chorus was: *"Tum jiyo hazaaro saal…"* which translates as "May you live a thousand years…" This song would often be played at birthday parties. Whenever I heard it, sadness would arise. Instead of making me happy it would make me sad, simply because it would ironically remind me of the short lifespan of my loved ones who were marching towards their deaths, me included! So, while it was being played at birthdays, and I would see others joyously sing along, it sent bells of doom ringing in my ears. And, even though the sentiment it aroused was heartwarming – may you live a thousand years – I thought it was quite absurd to hear someone sing some words that they knew deep down to be untrue. After all, who lives a thousand years? I wished we did, but knew that we don't.

I used to wonder: *What is the point of living if we are going to die one day? What is the point of enjoying pleasures if they are going to be snatched from us when we die? How could anyone be happy in such a scenario with the Grim Reaper or Yama, the God of Death, constantly looking over one's shoulder?*

Another vivid childhood memory I have is of a statue of Joan of Arc, which my mother had purchased from an antique shop in the hill town of Mussoorie. It was made of beautiful, white porcelain. However, I just couldn't figure out why she was tied to a stake, standing on a heap of wooden logs, and clasping a cross to her chest. What was going to happen to her? My mother explained that she was going to be burnt at the stake as they considered her a witch, even though she was a saint. I was horrified at that thought – that someone could be burnt alive! Years later, I read a theory that people at the stake didn't really suffer much, as the rising flames caused the blood to boil first and burst open the heart in no time – some consolation indeed! It was such an irony... a young, angelic-looking being propped up for this fate and frozen in eternity in the statue I used to look at every day. I remember reading an account that mentioned Joan's heart did not burn and was swiftly taken away to be thrown into the river lest it become a relic for worship. But, more of this later, as an essay emerged on St. Joan, which you will find later in this book.

A critical aspect of losing my father at a young age was that I clammed up. I tried to stop loving others simply because I knew I would eventually get hurt for they would die sooner or later. So, in order to prevent myself from getting hurt, the short cut was to stop loving others. This was actually a self-defeating proposition because it proved exactly the opposite – that it was in one's nature to love others, and to hold that love back required effort –

holding back the love only hurt 'me'! The situation became ironic: I had started building a wall to prevent others from hurting me, or rather, something happening to them from hurting me. However, this was going against my inherent human nature – to love others – and this wall was actually hurting me!

Through my formative years, fear, love and death were my inner companions, playing games with me in the playground of my mind. They were the three pieces of the jigsaw puzzle of life, and for the life of me, I just couldn't figure out how these pieces fitted together.

I often thought: 'We all grow up with this knowledge that we will die one day, yet it seems a distant reality.' It will indeed – simply because we do not know what it is to die – for we haven't died before in this life that we are living. So while we know what it feels like to lose a loved one, while the full knowledge of the inevitable end looms large for all our life, deep down we don't *feel* that we are going to die. Isn't this strange?

It was many years later when the understanding dawned that deep down, we don't feel we are going to die simply because… we don't. Deep down, we feel we will live forever simply because… we do. If we don't die, then *who* or *what* dies? And what lives forever? These questions, and more, were gradually answered during the years when I attended the talks of Ramesh Balsekar.

It was my good fortune that when I turned thirty, I came across a sage whose teaching was a validation of my life's experiences right from the time I could remember. I have herein referred to Ramesh as my guru, master, teacher – whatever term came spontaneously as the essays in this book emerged. These words are just labels for what can't really be given a name. He was my guru (which literally translates as 'one who dispels the darkness of ignorance'). He dispelled it by shining the spotlight of non-duality on my experiences. Just like a wild hare becomes immobile as its eyes get 'locked-in' when a searchlight is shone on it, likewise the teaching left me with no option but to view my life in the light of its clarity. Ramesh used to ask me to write as someone who has 'practised the teaching' in daily living. In these ways he became my teacher, but he was also my friend, philosopher, and guide.

Ramesh was a householder guru, which meant no orange robes or an ashram. He was a body builder in his younger days, a banker for thirty-seven years, a husband, father, grandfather, and great-grandfather. He was someone who was very accessible, who gave talks in his living room in South Mumbai to which seekers from all over the world flocked.

It was on being exposed to his teaching and that of his guru, Nisargadatta Maharaj, that the jigsaw pieces started to fit into place to eventually reveal one grand image. When I began reading books on talks with Maharaj, much of the content didn't make sense and yet the sentences hit home and had a deep impact. Some of his teaching went over my head but at the same time, it went under – straight to the heart. The reader will find a generous helping of references to both Ramesh's and Maharaj's teachings in this book. To avoid them would have required effort, as they 'came up' wherever and whenever they were meant to.

When I had just completed the manuscript of my most recent book on his teaching, Ramesh asked me to also include a piece about the terrorist attacks in Mumbai (26th November 2008) in light of the teaching of Advaita. I told him that it was too late as the book was already at the printers. Ramesh passed away in September 2009. After his passing, I found myself reading some of his earlier books that I had not read before. It's just as well that I hadn't because I would not have been able to comprehend a lot of the teaching at that time. It was during the months after he passed away that spontaneous essays started to emerge. These were based on many influences in my life – some significant and others seemingly insignificant – with the spotlight of the teaching now shining on them. Ramesh was interested in how the teaching impacted one's daily living, and not just the theoretical understanding of it. He referred to this as 'deliverance' – the understanding functioning in daily living. He would often say, "What use is any teaching if it does not impact one's daily living?"

There was no intention to bring these essays together in a book. However, as Ramesh had asked me to bring out the essay on the terrorist attack in my last book, it occurred to me that these essays could be brought together in a new book as they all focus one way or another on some aspect of the teaching of non-duality.

My publishing firm had helped organise events in Mumbai for the Synchronicity Foundation, USA. All of the members of the Synchronicity group were put up at one of the hotels where the attacks took place. They lost two beautiful beings – Alan and his young daughter Naomi – in the attacks. I had given Ramesh a detailed account of what transpired over those two days and nights during the attacks, as we were constantly in touch with Master Charles Cannon – Founder of Synchronicity – while he was confined in his room, just like many of the other members and hotel guests. We had gotten to know Alan well, as he had been coordinating all the event details with us over the preceding months. While there were six members of the group at the dining table (and all were shot at), it was Alan and his daughter who were destined to die that fateful night. The next few days were spent in hospital visits to inquire on the well-being of the other four members.

Ramesh perhaps thought that an intense experience like that would bring out aspects of the teaching that might be worth reflecting upon. He used to say, "Of what use is any teaching unless it can be tested in the fire of one's personal experience?" The indomitable Vimalananda expressed the same point differently when he said, rather brusquely, "What sort of educational system do we have nowadays? They announce their examinations in advance so that any idiot can mug up a bunch of notes in preparation. The key to testing someone is to test them when they least expect it and are least prepared for it. Then you have an accurate idea of how much they really know."* In any case, Ramesh had asked me to write about it and that is what came to pass – although almost two years later.

The writing here is simple. In fact, my first book *Pointers from Ramesh Balsekar* was nothing but a few paragraphs that covered the essence of the teaching, which took me all of two hours to put down. At the time,

---

* *Aghora – At the Left Hand of God*, Robert E. Svoboda, Rupa & Co.

I thought he might be quite disappointed when I had handed over the manuscript for him to read. When he returned it I said that I hoped he didn't mind that it was so short. He said, "Always remember… beauty in simplicity. That's the way it went in, so that's the way it came out."

There is no real sequence to the essays. You could read them in any order or you could read only some of them. If something you read here is meant to shine a light on some aspect of your life, then that is what would happen regardless of what you read or did not read. Some of the essays might just reflect a similar understanding when you view your life's events and situations through the prism of this teaching. This reminds me of a joke:

With a pile of three hundred résumes on his desk and a need to pick someone quickly, the boss told his assistant to make calls to the bottom fifty and toss out the rest. "Throw away two hundred and fifty résumes?" the assistant asked, shocked. "What if the best candidates are in there?" "You have a point," he said. "But then again, I don't need people with bad luck here."

If there is something you read in this book that moves you, so be it. For, that is what is meant to *be.*

Gautam Sachdeva
October 5, 2011

FORMS OF THE FORMLESS

An editor with one of India's leading newspapers once said to me that in Mumbai, one just needed to throw a stone and it would land in a guru's house. Although an exaggeration, the sentiment was perhaps valid for all of India. It doesn't stop just at gurus – psychics, astrologers, tarot readers, face readers, numerologists, shadow readers, palmists, you name it… our streets, lanes and by-lanes are full of spiritual and paranormal activity. I wonder if one can ever encounter such a variety anywhere else in the world.

It was while working on my mother's first book that I soon found myself being propelled into this intriguing new world – a world in which I encountered many spiritually gifted beings. I met them through a series of astoundingly synchronistic events. Somehow our paths crossed. I never sought out anyone as such but in spite of that the finding 'happened'. I would meet them through family and friends and, more often than not, through strangers. Initially, I had to be dragged to such meetings. I simply had no conscious interest in meeting them. But destiny had charted a different course for me, just as it was destined that I would be publishing spiritual books even though I had no interest in them at that time. It was only because we had a hard time finding a publisher for my mother's first book (it was an expensive book to produce as all her meditation illustrations were in colour), that I decided to publish it on my own. My background in advertising was of great help as I was familiar with the process of designing and printing. Once my mother's book was published more books followed and before I knew it, I was wearing the hat of a publisher of spiritual books.

Looking back, I am truly grateful for the twist in the journey that took me from advertising to publishing. I remember an incident in the early days when I was still in advertising. I was walking past the office reception area and saw an elderly lady conversing with the receptionist. She held a cake box in her hands. Intrigued, I went over and heard her tell the receptionist that she had read a book that had deeply impacted her. Since the author seemed to be living in another country, she had looked at the back of the book, found our address, and decided to come over to express her gratitude. That incident really touched me. I remember thinking that in all my years in advertising, our clients would consider it their way of saying thank you if they paid our bills on time! It gave me an additional impetus to focus more on book publishing. One really never knows the course that life takes and which events influence our lives. The cause and effect arrow is indeed double-pointed. I would not have taken the leap into publishing had it not been for my advertising background. In order for my career in publishing to happen, it was evident that first my career in advertising had to have happened.

This piece of writing is a brief account of some extraordinary beings I have met over the years who impacted me in one way or another. From each encounter there was something to learn. More often than not, it was a reaffirmation of what deeply resonated with my life's experiences and was a reflection of some aspect of my own master's teaching. This even includes the masters I met before meeting Ramesh Balsekar. When I look back, I can see what it was in those encounters that appealed to me, in light of the teaching of non-duality, even without having met Ramesh thus far.

Justice for all

Working on my mother's first book put me in touch with the first master I would meet on the spiritual path. It was her guru, Justice Dudhat. He gave talks at the college five buildings down the road from my home. A classroom had been generously provided by the college principal for the spiritual discourses, which took place once a week in the evenings. There are actually four colleges in the vicinity – not sprawling campuses like in the West, but four simple, box-like buildings, that are always in dire need of a paint job! I remember a joke that went around in the junior college claiming that we were all 'outstanding' students. Since there was hardly any campus except for the classroom corridors, we were standing out on the road most of the time, hence the moniker.

Justice Dudhat was a judge at the Bombay High Court. He used to conduct a course on Brahma Vidya (Knowledge of Brahman), the foundation of which was a set of breathing exercises based on an ancient Tibetan practice. He was totally committed to Brahma Vidya and would give weekly talks at four different locations in Mumbai. I attended his lectures, and started practising the breathing techniques. One of the sentences he often repeated during the talks, as well as at the weekly meditations at his home was: "Looking after you is the job of Totality." He would emphasise that the answer to any problem lay in Totality. Hearing that I would think, 'What a relief that is!' I never quite understood what the word Totality meant, but since it pointed to something much larger than 'me', it made Totality sound like a parent.

It was only years later that I got a clearer understanding of this word through Ramesh's writings. To summarise his words: 'In Totality, there is no duality of 'me' and the 'other'.' Totality is That which is prior to separation – the split of 'me' and the 'other'. In the waking state, the foundation of which is duality, Totality is the 'what is', in the moment, without the split of observer and observed in which the observer is constantly judging. In other words, it is duality as it is, without the *dualism* that is caused by the 'me' that considers itself *separate* from the 'other'.

Justice Dudhat was always very warm, welcoming and humorous. At the weekly meditations at his home, he would say to all of us, "This home is yours. Come any time you want. I am just a caretaker." On the rare occasions when I could make it from work to the meditations, he would look at me and say, *"Dekho dekho… Eid ka chand aa gaya!"* (Look, look… here comes the Eid moon). Since the festival of Ramzan Eid comes only once a year, he meant that I was making one of my rare 'once in a blue moon' appearances at his weekly meditations. He was well-built (having been a wrestler in his youth) and had a confident, charismatic and caring persona. He rarely spoke in the negative. During his last days, when someone asked him if he was uncomfortable, he replied, "It's not that I'm uncomfortable, but I'm not comfortable."

When I used to hear him tell people: "Leave all your problems here with me" (pointing at his feet), I would get startled. An internal dialogue would take place in my mind: *Is that for real? Will he work some magic? Of course not! How can he possibly solve everyone's problems? Then why is he saying it? Does he honestly think they will believe him?*

It was only later that the realisation dawned that it was perhaps one of the truest statements that could be made. For, as I read in one of Ramesh's earlier books, the guru is the Noumenon – the Source. I was analysing this statement from a dualistic individual perspective, when in truth there is no separation between the guru and the disciple. 'Leave your problems here with me' refers to the Source… not to a Guru 'me' that is separate from a disciple 'other'. Leave your problems with the Source. And what would happen in such a scenario? Invariably, the disciple would come back with much relief on his face. I really don't know if their external situation changed, but at least their attitude did. The relief experienced would be in direct proportion to the total surrender of the disciple to the Guru – a total relinquishing of the 'me and my problem' at the feet of the Source energy. Looking after you is indeed the job of Totality. The joker in the pack is that there is no 'you' to be looked after once surrender has happened, simply because it is the 'you' that has been surrendered.

Justice Dudhat passed away in 2005 after a brief illness. God must have truly been pleased to have him serve on the bench of life, dispensing justice as well as spiritual guidance to those who came within his ambit.

The river sage

I clearly remember the trip to Gagangiri Maharaj's ashram in Khopoli, on the outskirts of Mumbai. Amodini, the editor of my mother's first book, took us to meet him. She played interpreter, for we did not understand Marathi well. On an earlier trip, Amodini had taken my mother's diary of meditation sketches to show him. He had told her, "This is my subject. Bring them to me; I will guide them."

Prior to our meeting and seeking his blessings, he had instructed Amodini that we first visit his cave on the hill. Some call it the cave of the *Navnaths* (the nine revered Hindu saints). Once, on a visit to the ashram to meet Gagangiri, Dr. Ram Bhosle, the mystic masseur of Mumbai, had a vision of the Navnaths walking down from the cave and entering Gagangiri's room. However, when the doctor entered the room he did not find anyone there with the Master.

It was a desolate path to the cave, more of a muddy track really that wound through the forest. The earth below was full of crystal rock; we could see tiny crystals shining through the mud. Today, a concrete pathway has been built up to the cave for the convenience of climbers, but it takes away the charm. At that time, I recall a stray dog accompanied us up the track and into the cave as well. He was practically leading us, like a guide dog. After we came down and reached the ashram gate he quietly slipped away. It seemed as if he was assigned to be our guide.

We made our way to where Gagangiri was sitting in

the ashram on his swing. When our turn came to be introduced my mother showed him her final manuscript. He was engrossed in the drawings and, on seeing some, emitted a hearty laugh. It was an infectious laugh, like a child laughing in abandon. He was identifying with her experiences of the Kundalini energy and, in turn, explaining to her what she had drawn. He even gave us a recommendation letter for the first book.

When it was my turn to be introduced he interrupted Amodini and said, "I know him; you don't need to introduce us." He roughed up my hair as I bowed to offer him my *pranaams* (reverent salutations). I was quite thrilled to hear this but realised that no real 'conscious' benefit accrued from the statement as such, for he continued speaking to others and it seemed he was no longer aware of my presence. I remember hearing him saying, "Start your company!" It sounded more like an *aadesh* – a command. What was surprising was that I hadn't even mentioned to him that I was planning to start a company to publish my mother's book.

A few days after this trip, I mentioned to a friend that I had visited Gagangiri Maharaj. He looked at me and said, "Oh! I have to tell you something weird." He then went on to relate a story concerning his former girlfriend and the *jala yogi* (Gagangiri Baba's daily *sadhana,* spiritual practice, was to meditate in and under water). One day, the young woman had decided to take a walk near the river that flowed by the ashram. That particular area was forbidden territory as Gagangiri used to meditate in its waters and couldn't be disturbed. Seeing him sitting in the middle of the shallow but flowing river, she sneaked up to take a closer look. What she saw gave her a real fright for, when she looked at him, she saw three heads emerge from his head. She fled as if her feet were on fire. Gagangiri Maharaj, as I learnt later, was revered by his devotees to be a manifestation of Lord Dattatreya, the incarnation of Brahma-Vishnu-Mahesh, the presiding deity of the *sadhus* (holy men).

During his life spent undertaking intense spiritual practices in the wilderness, Gagangiri had experimented with the medicinal effects of wild herbs, roots and the healing properties of natural spring waters. The shepherds in those areas were among his earliest devotees. They were also his guides in healing, often bringing him the bark of special plants, roots and wild fruits from the forest as powerful anodynes for wounds and illnesses.

Gagangiri's solitary retreats to engage in *kayakalpa* – powerful periodic rejuvenation – were a part of the mystical lore that grew around him. He attained mastery over various healing techniques and nature cures as a result of the time he spent in the forests. He set up free herbal treatment facilities for chronic ailments like cancer and immune deficiencies in some of his ashrams spread across the Sahyadri Mountains.

Gagangiri Maharaj took samadhi in 2008. He was said to be a hundred and three years old at the time of his passing. Looking back, my first trip to meet him marked the beginning of something. Consciously, I didn't know what this 'something' was. Intuitively, I knew it was the start of a journey. Where the journey would lead, I had no clue.

Now I do. Home. This reminds me of a humorous

conversation I had with Chaitanya Balsekar, Ramesh's brother. He once told me, "Gautam, you're such a good person," to which I replied, "Thank you, but being good in this world doesn't get you anywhere." He promptly said, "Who said you have to go anywhere?"

In 2010, I was compelled to visit the ashram once again and pay my respects at the samadhi that has been built near the place where Gagangiri used to sit on his swing. Even though he is not present 'in his body', Gagangiri Maharaj has certainly not gone anywhere, for his powerful presence still graces the ashram.

The alchemist and his antiques

Patrick (name changed) has been a practising alchemist for decades. His home is a surreal setting with alchemical symbols subtly placed all over, a piranha pond in the compound (one you certainly wouldn't want to fall into), a lab straight out of a mystical, medieval novel – full of powders, beakers, liquids, solids and other forms of matter, and two large cabinets housing tomes on alchemy. He also boasts of a nice collection of exquisite Indian antiques, and therein lies an interesting tale.

The first time I visited my alchemist friend, I was fortunate to be given a tour of the room housing the antiques. It was a fascinating sight. Seeing that there were quite a few, I quipped that at least a couple could be fakes. I was standing on solid ground – he was French, and he had purchased them in India! He brushed my comment aside and continued with the guided tour. I mentioned it once again as I was browsing among the antiques and he said, "Impossible!" I commented that surely at least one of them might be a fake, as we have quite mastered the art of making fake antiques. What's more, it is fairly common that a gullible person easily falls prey to a devious manufacturer of fakes. Patrick brushed this comment aside in what seemed like a display of arrogance, saying that it was rather impossible that he might have a fake antique amidst his collection.

I thought his reaction was a bit uptight, and I indirectly expressed that he could do with learning the art of 'giving in' to a very real possibility, instead of living in his idealistic 'authentic antique collector' world. But he dug his heels in and refused to give in, reaffirming that each one of the pieces was authentic. A bit more gentle nudging from me, and he let loose. That was it! He had reached his tipping point and could take it no more. And so he explained, in a huff, how he staked his claim to the fact that each one of them was genuine.

Because of his intensive sadhana as an alchemist for many years, he had developed some unique gifts. One of them helped ensure that any antique he bought ought to be genuine. And this he ascertained without even touching the piece. For, if Patrick liked a particular piece, he would go into a meditative state and transfer his consciousness into the piece and then view the surroundings from that perspective: *Who was the sculptor sculpting it? What time period did he belong to? What clothes was he wearing? What tools was he using?* With this 'seeing' he could determine if the antique was genuine or he was being taken for a ride. All my arguments came to naught and fell like a house of cards. A skeptical mind could toss this out of the window. After all, where was the proof? I took it at face value and conceded the point. It was too far out not to believe in! Besides, his guru was a Siddha Yoga master of repute, so it was quite likely that as a dedicated disciple he received adequate training in the alternative arts.

I voiced the next thought that arose and asked him, "If you are able to transfer your consciousness into something as inanimate as stone, wouldn't it be easier to transfer it into something softer, say… another person, and check them inside out?" *Who has good intentions and who has bad ones? Who is a friend and who is a foe?* Patrick replied, with a mischievous twinkle in his eyes, "Well, *mon ami*, that's exactly what I did when you walked in through the door." He said he was joking, and I certainly hoped he was.

This encounter with Patrick clearly brought home the fact that an inanimate object may not seem to have consciousness, but Consciousness functions through all objects. Likewise, an animate object – say a human being – does not have consciousness; rather, Consciousness functions through the human object. Animate or inanimate, we are objects through whom Consciousness functions. What's more, the object itself is an appearance in Consciousness. One has to be conscious in order to perceive the object. So, in any case, an object cannot exist independent of Consciousness. So much for classifying objects as 'animate' and 'inanimate' when in truth they're only objects at the mercy of Consciousness, which alone determines whether they're animate or inanimate.

While *siddhis* (spiritual powers) can be a fascinating subject, Patrick would invariably point out an important aspect of the goal of alchemy – the philosopher's stone that is capable of converting base metal into gold. What needs to be realised is that the eternal principle 'as within, so without' applies. This really means that in the pursuit of the external goal, internal spiritual transformation would concurrently need to take place – the ultimate 'goal' being Enlightenment. Keeping this in mind, it would therefore mean that the Knights Templar, who were believed to have set up the European banking system and also built the most majestic sacred geometry cathedrals, were not the heretics on horseback they were made out to be. They had the ability to create alchemical gold, which is where their wealth supposedly came from, and one could therefore infer that they were perhaps spiritually evolved beings.

The next time you look at an antique, keep in mind that it might just be looking back at you. Just as it is an object in your consciousness, you are an object from the point of view of the Consciousness manifest within it. We're all objects through whom Consciousness functions. Consciousness does not label objects as animate or inanimate. It is we who do so. 'We', not as impersonal consciousness functioning through all the objects in the manifestation, but 'we' as individuals apparently separate from the objects that we perceive.

The psychic surgeon

The Rev. Alex Orbito, a famed psychic surgeon living in the Philippines, was conducting a seminar in Mumbai. It was attended by almost a hundred people. Over a half-day talk, he introduced us to the subject of psychic surgery. His method was based on a healing technique that translated as 'God, give your healing power to me'. He made us perform some light exercises, after which the surgeries commenced. We went in, one at a time, and each psychic surgery lasted up to a minute or so.

When it was my turn for the psychic surgery, I got onto the table, lay down and unbuttoned my shirt. The next thing I knew, he was gently poking around my stomach. And then, quite suddenly, his fingers slipped inside right up to his palm! He was feeling around... it was quite a strange experience. There was no pain, yet his hands had gone into what I thought would be uncharted territory – at least for his bare fingers. This lasted for about thirty seconds and before I could digest what was happening, the 'operation' was over. I looked at my belly... there was not a trace of what had seemingly transpired. He patted me on the cheek and the session was over. When I saw the video at home, I was quite amazed.

As he explained what psychic surgery was about, Rev. Orbito said that since the human body was 70 per cent water, his fingers or hands going into someone else's body should not be difficult to comprehend, for both bodies were nothing but two forms made up of 70 per cent water. Knowing what effects the phases of the moon have on the tides, one can't help but wonder what they must be doing to us whose bodies are made up of over two-thirds water. So much for thinking we're in control of all that we're feeling! Can you imagine, all that you think you are – some body with hopes, fears, aspirations, frustrations, grievances, regrets, expectations – is nothing but mostly water? Truly, we're not as solid as we seem – what a comforting thought! Take heart, there's no need to drown your sorrows; they're already drowned for their content itself is water!

Discussing the subject with people familiar with the healing sciences, I was informed that the operation as well as the healing was taking place at the 'subtle' level and not at the physical level. During various surgeries, Rev. Orbito would extract what seemed like a mass of dark red flesh. This was nothing but congealed and blocked energy that was being removed and not actual flesh – it was not being removed from the physical body. Even today when I watch the video, I can't seem to figure out what's happening. There have been some individuals who have given psychic surgery a bad name for they have been exposed as frauds. Nevertheless, my encounter with Rev. Alex Orbito and his seminar on psychic surgery was an enjoyable one. More than his skill set, I liked his youthful persona and lightness of being.

The subject of healing hands reminds me of my encounter with the mystic masseur.

The mystic masseur

I had heard of Dr. Ram Bhosle over the years. Some seekers who attended Ramesh's talks would end up going to Dr. Bhosle once the talks were over, as he stayed nearby on Malabar Hill where an affluent family had given him accommodation in a room in their palatial bungalow.

What drew me to Dr. Bhosle was his encounter with The Deathless One, Mahavatar Babaji, introduced for the first time to the world by Paramahansa Yogananda in his book *Autobiography of a Yogi*. 'Dr. Saheb', as Dr. Bhosle was fondly addressed, had murdered a British commandant who had committed atrocities against a woman in pre-independence India. The soldiers were out to get him so he fled to the Himalayas where a yogi gave him shelter. This yogi took care of all his needs, including his addiction to drink and drugs. Dr. Saheb had challenged his host, asking him if he knew the meaning of *atithi devobhava* – the guest is God. He had in effect said, "This is my daily diet, can you supply it? After all, one needs to treat one's guest as God." The yogi answered, "*Sab kuchh mil jayega*" (You will get everything). It was only later when he realised his host was none other than Babaji himself, that his addictions dropped off one by one. He ended up staying for six years in the Himalayas with Babaji.

Dr. Saheb had the gift of healing hands. The art of massage practiced by him was called *Samvahan*, which was a blend of ancient methods to bring the vibrational frequencies of the body into alignment. Bhagavan Nityananda of Ganeshpuri had told him that he would travel the world using his gift to heal people, and he undertook many such journeys. Among the personalities he is said to have healed were Mahatma Gandhi, Pandit Nehru, Churchill, Eisenhower and Bernard Shaw, to name a few. Nehru took it upon himself to send Dr. Saheb to various heads of state across the globe.

A few years ago, a friend of mine took me to meet Dr. Saheb. He was sitting up in his bed. He could not see much now as his eyesight was failing. He was a sweet, gentle and humble man in the winter of his illustrious life. All through our conversation, his fingers kept moving on the bed sheet as if in search of something to massage. It was such an incredible sight! It looked like his hands were powered by batteries, they seemed to have a will of their own and his fingers kept going on and on until he pulled them back.

I recall only two of the questions I asked him. The first was whether he had met Mahavatar Babaji in Mumbai. He answered that he indeed had, and that too on several occasions. My next question was if he could sum up in one sentence all that life had taught him. He replied, "God exists between the R and the M of RAM."

Coincidentally, Shirish Bhagwat, who I knew personally, was the surgeon who operated on Dr. Saheb towards the end of his life. Dr. Saheb had told Shirish that when he was admitted in the hospital a few years ago, he had seen *Mahakala* (The Lord of Death in the form of Time) hovering outside the window. He then said, "But he (looking at the picture of Babaji near his bed) said that it was not yet my time." When I told Shirish what Dr. Saheb had said about God existing between the R and M of RAM, he said it reminded him of this legend:

At one time, Hanuman's * *ego got bloated. After all, he was the one to to have discovered where Sita was being held captive and had soon after burnt down the entire city of Lanka. He went and asked Lord Ram if there was anything at all left for him to do. Seeing Hanuman's chest swell with pride, Lord Ram asked Hanuman to do him a favour. He wanted someone to cover all the universes, and said he thought of no candidate more worthy than Hanuman for this task. Hanuman was even more elated to hear this – to be told that he was considered the only one capable of taking on this endeavour. He asked Lord Ram, "But how will I know that I have covered all the universes?" The Lord said that at the end of all the universes he would find three pillars. When he*

* Hanuman was a Vanara, belonging to a mythical race with simian attributes, and was the chief devotee of Lord Ram.

saw them, he was to mark a cross on them and then return. Off went Hanuman, roaming the galaxies. Universes began and universes ended, and Hanuman journeyed on. Lo and behold, he finally came to three pillars and was overjoyed at the sight. He promptly marked a cross on each pillar and, his task accomplished, embarked on his return journey. He presented himself before Lord Ram and proudly declared that he had found the three pillars. The Lord then raised his hand... three fingers had crosses marked on them. He asked Hanuman if that is what he had seen. Hanuman was humbled; it was then he realised that all universes begin and end with Ram.

The sun yogi

India truly knows how to shake up what one could consider 'conditioned reality'. You never know what or who you might see or encounter next. Anything is possible in this land of infinite possibilities. Light doesn't travel only in straight lines here, it bends at unimaginable arcs, which our limited mind and intellect simply can't fathom. The subject of light brings me to my unforgettable encounter with a yogi who is a devout worshipper of the sun.

He looked like an Indian Jesus, and was someone I took to immediately. One evening, he invited a few of us to a *yagna* (sacred fire ritual), which we performed on the terrace of his ashram. This was in the suburbs of Mumbai. At one point, during the fire ceremony, he asked us to close our eyes and not open them until instructed to do so. Several minutes passed and, wondering what was happening, I decided to subtly open my eyes to check out the scene. Everyone was sitting quietly with their eyes closed, including the yogi himself. Then, something most peculiar happened... I saw his form begin to fade away. Little by little it vanished, until I could only see the wall that was behind him. I looked around and everyone else was exactly as they were – sitting with their eyes closed. It was only his form that had disappeared, so I knew I was not hallucinating. Then, after a minute or so, I saw his form gradually take shape and return. I quickly closed my eyes lest I be 'caught' by him, and waited for his permission to open our eyes again.

At another time, there was a Sun Yoga session being conducted on Chowpatty Beach in South Mumbai. About twenty of us had assembled there. When the Sun Yogi came, all the stray dogs on the beach went ecstatic with joy – they ran to him, tails wagging, yelping, and playfully tugging at his (until then) spotless white *lungi**. When the session began, it soon started raining. There was nowhere to run as we were right in the middle of the beach. Suddenly, the rain stopped. However, it continued raining all around us, fifteen feet away.

After the Sun Yoga session he came home for breakfast, which consisted of fruit and milk. We got along very well. It was like being with someone familiar – an old friend. He said, "I keep telling people, don't treat me like a guru. Treat me as a friend." He was young, raw, and not used to the adulation and awe heaped upon him. When I recently spoke to him, he had taken his yoga to schools and universities across Asia and was heading to Europe.

Talking of Europe brings to mind Louis XIV who was known as *Le Roi-Soleil*, the Sun King. He built the palace of

* A single piece of cloth, around three metres in length, wrapped around the waist and covering the legs.

Versailles in France, one of the most lavish and opulent palaces ever built in the whole wide world. It was known as The Palace of the Sun King. However, as with all material things, the palace eventually fell into decay when the king's coffers emptied. As the saying goes, 'Decay is inherent in all things'. When I visited Versailles what I enjoyed more were the palace gardens rather than the palace itself. Nature's grandeur has a way of overpowering even the most opulent of man-made structures.

India's sun kings are in stark contrast; such is the duality in this manifestation as we know it. Their body, the temple of the living god, is their palace and through the mastery of Sun Yoga, the sun sits on the throne. India worships emperors who radiate Light!

And so, over the years, these meetings with the masters were a direct confirmation that forms are not as solid as they appear to be. Or rather, forms are not what they appear to be – something we all have often heard or read. Whether it was Gagangiri, Patrick, Rev. Alex Orbito or the Sun Yogi, one thing was clear: the certainty of what one perceived as real was no longer tenable.

It had lost all verdicts in the hallowed courts of logic and reason.

It had flowed away with the river in Khopoli.

It had been yanked out of the body-mind with bare hands.

It had been burnt to ashes by the sun's rays.

Yogiraj Gurunath, a dynamic Kriya Yoga master, mentioned to me that once when he bowed down to touch the divine Anandamayi Ma's feet, his hands went right through and hit the ground. I have always enjoyed meeting Gurunath. Whether he is reciting poetry, narrating anecdotes of the famed *Nath** yogis, and even when he's 'needling' me, he's 'full on' enjoying every bit of it. One of Gurunath's quotes that I like is: "Right from the moment of birth, the heresy of separation occurs."

Of course, one of the first things to happen to a baby after it is born is that the parents give it a name. The separation thus gets even more entrenched as there is a name given to the form, which now responds to its name being called. This brings me to the next story.

The master of the moment

In 2004, a group of us – family and friends – met Eckhart Tolle in Glastonbury, UK. He was there to give a talk on his way to Findhorn in Scotland. We met him the evening before his talk, over dinner. I remember introducing some friends to him and when the introductions were done with, he looked at me and said, "Thank you for the introductions… and who might you be?" and we both followed it with a laugh. There was something about that moment that stayed with me. Of course, it was evident that what he was pointing to, even in jest, was that I had just introduced people with their names, which is not who they were in their true essence. I remember that sentence playing itself over in my head while we were sitting with him on the lawns of the house, not because it was a profound one, but because it was a clear example of how simple statements have such

---

* An ancient lineage of spiritual masters. Its founding is traditionally ascribed to Lord Dattatreya.

obvious meanings that we totally miss in this realm of separation and identification. Each time the sentence played over, the emphasis was being placed on a different word – it was like a booby-trap for the ego.

And *who* might you be?
And who *might* you be?
And who might *you* be?
And who might you *be*?

The answer was in the question itself. *Who* is the *you*? Consciousness, not the form of the body and the name given to it – but the animating presence without which you would not *be*. Nisargadatta Maharaj would tell visitors coming to him not to talk and ask questions as one individual to another, but as consciousness to consciousness. What he meant was that they should not pose questions taking themselves to be separate individuals identified with their bodies. The 'might' that Eckhart used was a gentle slice from a sword that opened up another dimension. Had he said, "Who are you?" the ego would have promptly replied, "Gautam!" And then, the musings on that sentence might not have happened.

What I enjoyed most while being with Eckhart was that I found someone who loved silence as much as I did. The high points of meeting him centred on the fact that there was hardly any talking. I remember being a very quiet child. In school I had even got a white card for the 'most well behaved and quietest boy in class'. It was quite embarrassing at the time. I remember the times when I would sit quietly and people would think something was wrong with me. "What are you thinking?" they would come up and ask. And then I thought it was perhaps wrong to be quiet and silent. This was the conditioning I grew up with. I even remember the thought that would arise in my mind, 'I sit quietly and don't bother people, and now it seems that they are bothered by the fact that I don't bother them! Should I be saying or doing something all the time?' Of course, this does not mean that I would just sit and 'not think' all the time. A lot of thinking happened; worry and fear were my childhood friends. But, there were many occasions when I was just sitting and not thinking, which somehow seemed to be an abnormal mode of behaviour to others.

A curious incident took place at one of Ramesh's talks some years ago. A couple had come with their beautiful little girl who must have been about six years old. She sat quietly on the swing of the living room, and appeared to be enjoying herself, swinging gently, observing the people and looking out of the window. What a peaceful expression this child had on her face! It certainly didn't look like a forced silence, one that she had been forced to maintain on account of a disciplined and regimented upbringing. After the talks were over, somebody went over to her parents and said the child was not normal for children her age should be running around and creating a ruckus. The parents were quite perplexed at this remark and, not knowing how to respond to this unsolicited advice, just nodded their heads and gave an awkward smile. When I looked back at the child, she was happily conversing with all those who went up to her. She did not shy away, or go into a cocoon; there were no barriers, as such, in place. I went up to the father and remarked that his child seemed like a little Buddha, and he said she had been like that ever since he could remember. It is so clear that if a child's nature is one of quietude, there is no point in trying to change it to fit a conventional image of what a child should be like. It only confuses the child more as he or she is being asked to act against what comes naturally – just like a child who is naturally inclined to use his left hand is forced by a parent to use his right hand.

It is incredible how one's basic personality stays the same over the years. One day, Ramesh introduced me to his grandnephew and told me, "I've been wanting to introduce the two of you. He is a quiet boy, like you." And this 'boy', meaning I, was almost thirty-nine at the time!

While there was not much talking with Eckhart, there was a lot of walking. He loved to walk. Whether it was climbing up the Glastonbury Tor, walking on the dry Findhorn riverbed, climbing up Arunachala Hill, or through the forest behind his home in Vancouver, we took long walks where only silence was exchanged – not words. What a relief! When our group planned to visit the Glastonbury Tor, we had booked a tour guide. When I mentioned this to Eckhart, he said that he was not interested in dates and history-related details that one normally gets on a tour, and so would excuse himself (perhaps one couldn't expect any other response from the author of *The Power of Now*). Unless we chose to have him take us up the Tor as our tour guide, although it would be a silent walk up in order to soak in the atmosphere of the sacred hill. Was there even a choice?

Eckhart is like a ford-crosser. He took the subject of non-duality and brought it to the masses. The gap was bridged. For the ego, it had to appear that one could *do* something to be in the present moment. In reality, there is only Presence: Presence that is there prior to you knowing that you are present as an individual. How could you be present were it not for Presence – impersonal Presence? How could 'I am Gautam' come prior to 'I am'? I am – the impersonal awareness of being, of Presence – the force that operates through all of us. In fact, Presence is nothing but the absence of the individual 'you' who thinks he is present. Once the 'you' steps in and claims 'I am present', presence has become personalised – 'I as a separate entity am present'. What was an impersonal Presence is now objectified, with the separate individual staking claim to being the one who is present. Eckhart has tricked the ego into believing there is something it can do to be present. It is easier to work with the ego, rather than tell someone they have to annihilate the ego – which in any case is an impossibility as it means telling the ego to annihilate itself! He thus upholds the grand Trickster archetype in the mythologies of the world. The Truth is eventually delivered and a splendid job is done of it.

When we were sitting on the lawns that evening, someone mentioned to Eckhart that it was believed that the last resting place of the Holy Grail was Glastonbury. Eckhart chuckled and said, "It's perhaps behind me, in the bush!" This reminds me of one of my favourite French sayings: *Vous ne trouvez pas le Saint-Graal. C'est le Saint-Graal qui vous trouve* (You do not find the Holy Grail; it is the Holy Grail that finds you).

Ramesh used to define the ego as 'identification with a name and form as a separate entity'. His definition reminds me of a recent incident. I had been invited to a tea party. A lady got into an animated conversation with me. She was narrating an incident that reconfirmed that she was being looked after by a Higher Power as it was a miraculous escape that she had made in a car accident. All through this monologue she kept referring to me as Gaurav (or Girish... I can't recall). In any case, she was not referring to me as Gautam. She was going on and on... "You know Gaurav, what happened next... and then, Gaurav, you won't believe it... can you imagine, Gaurav..." I thought it was quite funny. Of course, my immediate reaction was 'Hey, that's not my name' but I did not voice it. I was quite engrossed in her narration and thought I should not break her stream of words, for she was like a car in fifth gear! In any case, what difference would it have made to the story? At the end of the party when I was about to leave, she came up to me visibly upset. She said, "Oh, you did not tell me your name is Gautam! Every time I mentioned your name wrongly you did not correct me! You should have corrected me! I am so sorry..." and so on. I smiled and told her exactly what I felt. "It was the narration of the story I was engrossed in, and my name was irrelevant to it."

She had a look of disbelief on her face. It seemed it was the strangest thing she had heard. It struck me as to how deeply identified we are with people's names, including our own. I am not propagating that you let people call you any name they wish, that would create a heap of names when even one is more than we can handle. But the next time someone calls you by a name other than your own, see how quickly the identification comes up to defend your so-called real name, who you *think* you are.

Immense gratitude arises whenever the memory of my time with Ramesh comes up, for he lifted this veil of identification and exposed the Divine fraud of separation.

The enlightened banker

There are enough accounts perhaps to write a book on these fascinating encounters – from yogis who sucked out cancer cells to face-readers who could identify a culprit by just looking at the faces during a line-up of suspects. While I did learn a lot from all these enriching meetings, I still found that I returned every Sunday to Ramesh's home. Perhaps this was because while I saw many miracles and met beings with siddhis, for me, Ramesh had, and spoke about, the greatest siddhi of them all: peace of mind in daily living.

Ramesh used to say in his talks, "What will enlightenment give you that you did not have before? The ability to walk on water? No. The ability to be in two places at the same time? No. The ability to find a car pulling out of the parking spot at the same time you want to park your car? Forget it! All enlightenment will do for you is give you peace of mind in daily living."

Speaking about occult powers, Meher Baba said, "Through different yogas one can attain strange, occult powers such as walking on water… All these different powers attained through yoga practices are phenomenal, and hence, transient and unreal. These have nothing to do with spirituality or spiritual powers, which are already latent in all but manifest only in a few select ones who have realised the Self."*

---

* *Lord Meher*, Bhau Kalchuri, Vol. 8, p. 2959, Sheriar Press.

And so, I am grateful that while my feet took me off on a tangent now and then, at the same time they were planted knee-deep in the cement of the teaching of non-duality. The second time I had gone to visit Ramesh, he told me, "You've come again, have you? Be careful, this place could become your Sunday church." Little did I know that his words would come true for almost ten years, right up to the time he passed away.

The strangest thing is that the first time I went to one of his talks, I got thoroughly bored and thought it was strange that people from all over the world should come to a household in Mumbai to listen to someone say that everything was the will of God! I went each subsequent weekend to see what it was that I hadn't got, and that's how the journey began. You never know where you really land up and what course events take. That's because it's never 'you' who really lands up, the 'landing up' happens; 'you' are just incidental to the events that take place. It was a few months after visiting him that, one day, as I was browsing the book shelves at my home, I was surprised to find Ramesh staring at me from the cover of one of the books. It was one of his earlier books called *Consciousness Speaks*. My mother had been gifted it a while ago. It was only then that it struck me that it was the same sage that I had started visiting.

The beauty of Ramesh's teaching was in its simplicity. That is what appealed to me the most. His mantra was "Everything is a happening; nobody does anything." It was deeply profound, at the same time the Divine role of demolishing the sense of 'doership' in the ego played at its core.

What was also endearing was that he was down-to-earth and easily accessible. He was your regular Indian grandpa, wearing a white *kurta-pyjama**, sitting in a rocking chair in his living room with us gathered around him. The postman would ring the doorbell, the pressure cooker would go off in the kitchen, the noise of the car honking on the street below would filter up to the room. It was an ordinary Mumbai household in which the daily talks took place.

When I first met him, Ramesh had a colourful life of eighty-three years behind him. He had been a body-builder in his younger days, a banker for thirty-seven years with one of India's leading banks, and had seen the ups and downs of life as we know it, including the pain of losing a son. Everything about him was 'ordinary' and one could relate to it easily. In his biography *The Happening of a Guru,* he said, "It did not take me long to discover my ordinariness... My ordinariness, I must admit, was not a 'C' ordinariness but, rather, a 'B+' ordinariness."

Over the years I met many astrologers who predicted the future. Being on the spiritual path, and moreso as a spiritual publisher, encountering them is a common occurrence. Some were brilliant and some weren't; some were vaguely accurate on most things but not all. Some were very accurate on a few things but not most. Some were accurate some of the time; some were accurate most of the time, but none were accurate all of the time. It was all so individualistic and relative. I would meet someone who would say, "So-and-so is brilliant, go and see her." Then I would meet someone else who would say, "Don't bother

---

* Traditional dress of men in India.

meeting that lady; whatever she told me didn't come true." If anyone asked me about anyone, assuming I knew something about everyone connected with the spiritual path in India, my answer was, "You should go and find out for yourself." I would follow this approach even when I would meet spiritual masters or authors. There were always two or more opinions floating around. The only way forward was to see things for oneself.

The subjects of predicting the future and that of destiny bring to mind gemstones. Recommending them is a passion of astrologers since wearing them is an intrinsic 'remedial measure' of Vedic astrology. Some recommended a yellow sapphire, some a blue, others a ruby, and still others an emerald, and yet others, a diamond. Some suggested wearing a yellow sapphire on the ring finger of the left hand, others on the index finger of the right hand. Some said to get the ring made in gold, others suggested silver, while others said the ring had to be made of white gold. Some said the carats had to be more than your age, others said the carats didn't matter but the colour of the stone did; some said the colour should be pale, others said the colour should be dark. I remember buying or being gifted some stones. If some astrologers had their way, I would have to wear one on each finger. Mercifully, my collection was limited to three. So what do I do now that these stones have been recommended? I have always liked the hues of gemstones, and I wear what I like to wear, what I feel comfortable with. That's perhaps not strictly following the protocol, but that's what seems to happen with me. More often than not, I find myself wearing none.

It's the same with visiting temples. I have never been

one for rituals or temples, but one day the feeling arose that I must experience this aspect, which is also an integral part of Indian culture. I started visiting a *Shani* (Saturn) temple on *Shanivar* (Saturdays). I began to enjoy the visits, but some days I was forcing myself to go. I had a friend who would religiously go to various temples on the appointed days. He would have a sleepless night if he missed a day. While I am quite disciplined and can easily slip into a routine, I did not have this burning desire, even though I ended up going almost every Saturday for two years. Now, when I feel like going, I go. When I don't, I don't. But what I do is that on the day I don't end up going, I sit on my bed and visualise myself in the temple… it is such fun! For the imagination is limitless. I 'photoshop' the crowds out from the visual and it's just me standing in front of the statue of Shani Dev. Then, I picture myself presenting a gigantic vat of oil, the prescribed offering, and pouring it gently on the statue. Usually, one gets a small bowl filled with oil just outside the temple. But this way, my offering is limitless – I could offer a thousand gallons. Other visuals sometimes get added on their own accord. Whatever comes up spontaneously, like a dozen coconuts being offered, or a cascading shower of flowers. For the imagination is a field of limitless possibilities.

Another aspect of the temple visits was that I never knew what to ask for. The same friend that I mentioned earlier was clear that he wanted a Louis Vuitton bag and so prayed to get it (and get it he did, in his case). All I used to ask for was the strength to deal with life's situations, and the health of loved ones, myself included. I used to think, 'What's the point of asking for something if you don't know whether or not it's good for you in the first place? What may be 'good' today may not be 'good' tomorrow'.

Coming back to the teaching, given all the complexities involved with the future, what better balm is there than to be told, "If something is to happen then no power can prevent it from happening, and if something is not meant to happen then no power on earth can make it happen."

I am grateful to God that it was my destiny to have met a master whose teaching resonated with me from the core of my heart, for it was my life's experience. His concept was that everything is predestined; destiny is stamped at the moment of conception. For him, everything was predestined and etched in stone. Not the stone that you wear on your finger, but the stone that was the rock-solid understanding that led to peace of mind in daily living.

Now, where can you buy such a stone? What colour is it? How many carats? Which finger do you wear it on? Do you set it in gold or silver?

In the horoscope of your life, there is one thing for certain that I see – you will never know what the next moment will bring – pleasure or pain. It could be your friend calling to say his wife just delivered a baby boy and they decided to make you the baby's godfather, or it could be the news that a loved one was killed in a terrorist attack. Something will surely happen. Where and what it will lead to, God alone knows. Knowing this, visit all the temples you feel like visiting and worship the gods with abandon, bedeck yourself with all the stones that Mother Earth has to offer from the depths of her treasure trove, rejoice in the inevitability of the inevitable, knowing that it could be no other way – for if it could have, it would have.

LESSONS FROM THE LITTLE TEACHER

I had known him since he was two months old. He had never seen his father, and was taken away from his mother as she was unable to look after all her children. She simply did not have the resources to handle five children on her own.

He was the quiet sort. He didn't like to speak much. And when he did, it was hard to understand what he was saying. He was a special child of God. You could say he had been denied 'the dubious gift of intellect'. Perhaps that was a gift as far as he was concerned. For it meant he didn't ask "Why?" … a question that plagues most of us. *Why was I born? What am I doing here? What is my purpose? Why did he say this to me? Why did she do that? Why don't things go the way I want? What will happen to me?*

His foster family took good care of him. They did not send him to school, as there was none in the town for those like him. As a result, he didn't have many friends and ended up spending most of his time at home. What he enjoyed most was being taken outdoors for long morning walks by the seaside. He loved the outdoors, and what really got him excited was knowing the time for his walk had arrived. He could not read the time but knew exactly when it was time and would be ready and waiting at the door.

On the promenade, he would be running ahead as if he had discovered freedom, happily leaving his guardian behind until his name was called out. Then he would reluctantly make his way back.

What I found endearing was his simplicity. All that seemed to matter to him were the 'basics' of life – food, sunshine, sleep, and an occasional hug. He needed so little to keep himself happy. I had rarely seen him sulk. You could say he was an introvert. He did not have many friends, and did not engage in unnecessary dialogue with the few he had. I used to wonder whether he liked people at all, or just put up with them because he was forced to interact with them. Of course, as with all children, he was all over you if you got him a gift – especially if it was ice cream. You then became one of his favourite people in the world. Until the ice cream got over, that is.

He seemed to be a shining example of living in the present moment. So much has been written about this, but here was a living embodiment of the same. No one had told him about 'being in the present', nor was he of an age or intellectual calibre to understand such concepts. Yet, I don't remember him mentioning anything at all about a past hurt or a future fear. None of that seemed to arise in his mind. I never heard him asking his guardian about any 'tomorrow', or complaining about a 'yesterday'.

Talking about fear, there was an interesting encounter I had with fear, or rather, fear had with me. One day, I was in the office and the phone rang on my desk. I took the call and received some work-related news that was not very pleasant. In that instant when the news filtered into my ear through the receiver, I sensed the fear rise. It came up from somewhere near the base of the spine, climbed up till the heart area, and then fell back down. I was astonished. All this happened in a trice, and yet it seemed to occur in slow motion. There was something that was witness to this sensation of fear that rose and then fell. I realised how instinctive a fear 'reaction' is, be it a physical or a psychological fear. Sometimes it seems there is a very thin, blurred line between the two. Physical fear is an auto-mechanism, else we would be crossing the road without looking left or right. It is something with which we are programmed. With psychological fear, it seems we are more involved in the fear, which is more often than not over-amplified as compared to the situation.

Psychological fear is more about the fear of the survival of 'me' as a separate entity, operating in the duration of time. The 'me' totally identified with the body as a separate entity, fears for its existence at some point in the future. However, the fact is that we did not create the 'me' in the first place, so how could 'we' create psychological fear? A psychological fear may arise if it is meant to, depending on the nature of the person in whom the fear arises. However, 'the difference' to paraphrase Ramesh, 'between the sage and the ordinary person is that the sage does not get *involved* in the fear, and witnesses the fear arising in a 'body-mind organism' that happens to be his, in this case'. In the instance I just described, the fear was witnessed as a wave that rose and fell 'in the moment'. However, if there was an involvement in the fear, the wave-sensation-emotion of fear would perhaps have spread throughout the body, into muscles, tissues, etc., creating tension and imbalance in the body system and its functioning. This is a likely outcome when one is in the grip of fear and cannot escape its clutches.

How can I be less fearful? The question itself is misconceived. To try to be less fearful is a further involvement in the fear, diametrically opposite to one's supposedly good intention. It's just human nature that we can't leave fear alone, and let it be.

So here was this little one, totally in the Now. Perhaps he would worry about the future if the roof above his head was gone, or his next meal did not arrive on time… there was no way of knowing. Whenever he was asked if anything was on his mind, he would simply give a blank look as if he didn't understand what we meant, and then he looked away with complete disinterest. In fact, it seemed as if something was wrong with the questioner to have asked such a question. He was such a content being that it was a joy to be around someone like him – somehow the air felt lighter. We all used to call him 'our little enlightened one'.

Coming back to his relationship with people, he had a most interesting one with the spiritual master who would come over to his foster family's home once a week. A gathering of about fifteen to twenty people used to take place at the home. The group would get together for a meditation led by the master. He didn't really care for the group, some of whose members were genuinely fond of him while others thought he was a bit weird and tried to keep their distance, acting on some subconscious fear in their minds. But what was fascinating to watch was that the moment the meditation would begin, he would quietly enter the living room, go right up to where the master sat and sit at the feet of the master throughout the duration of the meditation. After about half an hour, the minute the master uttered a long drawn out "Om" to signal the end of the meditation, he would immediately get up and leave the room. No verbal communication took place between him and the master, and it was a mutual understanding between them that none was required. It seems like these special children of God are directly connected to Him; there is something deeply spiritual about their very existence. We could learn so much from them.

He had to be taken at regular intervals to the doctor for his check-ups. He disliked these visits and a sneaking suspicion that he was heading to the place he least liked would set in when he would recognise the approach as he sat in the car. The doctor, though, loved him and took good care of him. While he had a more than healthy existence for somebody of his kind, it was believed that he would only live till eleven or twelve years of age. It was rare for anyone like him to make it beyond this age. However, he lived on to see seventeen summers.

I think one main factor that contributed to his extended lifespan was the food he ate. He was almost like a sadhu – he ate the same healthy food day in and day out without a complaint, except for the occasional ice cream. All meals were fed to him lovingly and on time. His food was made as per what the doctor recommended as his daily diet, and what his young body could digest. He ate just about the amount necessary, and there were times when he would decide to fast and not eat for a couple of days in a row. The doctor said not to worry about it as long as he did not display any undue signs of fatigue. It seemed he was totally tuned in to his body rhythms and perhaps decided it was time for fasting in order to cleanse his system. Of course, whenever we asked him what the matter was, he would not reply. He was, you could say, 'a man of few words'. If only we all could exercise such intuition with our food intake.

And so, seventeen years passed by. Towards the end, his eyesight became weak and he started bumping into furniture. He went for shorter walks as his stamina was decreasing. He wasn't as sprightly as before. He even began to eat less. But barring this, he was hale and hearty. He never had to be taken to the hospital once. I happened to be with him the day he passed away at home. It was quick. He took three long breaths, and then it was over – it seemed like a cardiac arrest. No more breathing. There was no point in calling the doctor.

Was a life of seventeen years short? Of course it was. But then, considering that the expected lifespan was supposed to be twelve, it had, by the grace of God, been extended by 50 per cent in his case. Could one ask for more? We really ought to be grateful to God for whatever time we get to spend with our loved ones. We simply take each day of their existence for granted and only feel their loss when they are gone from our lives. We were all worried whether he would make it till twelve, and here he was comfortably chugging along till seventeen. He never once mentioned that he loved us, but we knew he did. You see, quite a few of us do not express the love we feel towards another, for fear that the love is not returned, or for a hundred other reasons. But this was not so in his case. For while God didn't make him so expressive, what gave him away was that when he would see you and was happy, he couldn't help but wag his tail, or rather, his tail wagged him.

If only God had gifted tails to human beings.

Notes:

Jeffrey was our miniature daschund. My eldest sister Shibani decided to name him Jeffrey when we got him, after Jeffrey Archer, who was her favourite author at the time. He loved my mother the most since she took him for his walks on Marine Drive.

This essay is inspired by a short story in Jeffrey Archer's book called *Just Good Friends* (from the book *A Twist in the Tale* – Hodder & Stoughton) that I had read when I was eighteen.

Thank you Jeffrey… and Jeffrey.

Ramesh Balsekar would often say that animals do not have the dubious gift of intellect, which makes the human being ask questions.

WHERE YOU ARE MEANT TO BE

In 2006, my friend Hersh and I decided to visit the Spiritual Centre while we were in London. Nan Umrigar, one of the authors published by my firm, had referred to it in her book *Sounds of Silence*. When I informed Nan that I was travelling to London, she was keen that I visit the Centre as she had had a good experience there. So when we were planning the details of our trip, I suggested it to my friend and he readily agreed. We checked the address and other details on the website, and after going through the schedule of events, decided the date on which we planned the visit to the Centre during our stay there.

In London, we got hold of a map of the Tube and set off for the Spiritual Centre situated at 33, Belgrave Square. Locating it wasn't quite that simple, for neither of us had visited that part of London before. We had to ask around a bit but eventually found the place and arrived there well in time. The event we had chosen to attend was a meeting with a clairvoyant – a public demonstration of his abilities. We paid our fees at the reception desk and were shown where to go. In the room, we settled into our seats. There were just a handful of us, and the clairvoyant started to give each one of us a reading based on the messages that came to him.

He had a nice air about him – he was a simple man who spoke clearly and to the point. He was, for the most part, uncannily accurate as far as the readings for my friend and I were concerned. He even mentioned that I seemed to be attending some kind of a 'school of philosophy' on a regular basis, and that it was a good place to visit as he got the impression of a lot of light emanating from there. Of course, I knew he was referring to my teacher's *satsangs* (spiritual gatherings) that I was attending. It wasn't exactly a school of philosophy… more like talks that my teacher had with visitors in his living room. But I understood that the clairvoyant was framing the image in the context with which he was familiar. Anyway, not that one needed it, but it was a validation that I was spending quality time at the right place.

After the session was over, we left quite satisfied. It was an afternoon well spent.

Three years later…

In 2009, I was once again holidaying in London. A friend of mine from America happened to be there at the same time. I gave him a call one morning and as he was relatively free that day, we decided to meet for lunch. Neither of us knew London too well. We met at Green Park, strolled around a bit, reached Buckingham Palace, and then were clueless as to where to go for lunch. As we walked past Buckingham Palace I remember thinking that the guards were so wonderfully still despite their uncomfortable uniform and headgear, as if they were undercover yogis in different states of samadhi! Ambling along, we chanced upon a nice Italian restaurant and decided to eat there. After the meal we had some time to spare and took a walk around the picturesque neighbourhood. About twenty minutes into the walk, I sensed that I was in familiar territory and before I knew it, we were standing right in front of the door of… 33, Belgrave Square!

Rather pleased at this coincidence, I suggested to my friend that we step in. As he was a healer by profession, I thought perhaps there was a reason why we were there, and it might be a good idea for him to meet the people running the Centre. He could connect with them as they were involved in similar work. As soon as we entered, the person at the desk asked us to hurry up as we were late for the public demonstration. He said that since we were just five minutes late, he could let us in. I was quite surprised at the way events were unfolding. Neither of us had planned for this; we had not intended to come here for a reading. We looked at each other, shrugged, paid the fee, walked in and… to my surprise, it was the same clairvoyant I had met three years ago! What's more, he had not yet begun the session. As we slid into our seats at the back, everyone turned around to look at the two new entrants who had disturbed the peace. Then the clairvoyant decided to begin the session and of all people, the first person he pointed to was… me! But, this is not about the reading.

This coincidence of being at 33, Belgrave Square again gave me a valuable insight; it was something I had always known deep within, and I think that we all know it. You will be exactly where you are meant to be at a given point in time. In the first instance, in my case, we did all the planning we could and ended up at our destination. In the second, we did no planning at all yet we landed up there. What was even clearer was that to be at 33, Belgrave Square the first time required some planning; to be there the second time, required no planning.

The 'planning' was clearly just a mechanism for the first trip to happen. It would be silly to assume that 'I' did the planning, for the plan to go there was based on the fact that someone had suggested that I would do well to visit the Centre. If I had not received that suggestion, I would not have planned the first trip. What's more, there had to be a trigger for someone suggesting that I go there. There had to be something that had made Nan go there in the first place in order for her to recommend it to me. And that something itself depended on another cause-effect loop. One could trace this back endlessly in an arc of perpetual regression and find that a series of seemingly unrelated events lead one to exactly where one is supposed to be at a given point in time, physically or emotionally. When that string of events actually began – at which point of time – would be anyone's guess! It could have begun a day ago or a hundred years ago. Where it ends is clear – here and now – which, of course, will be the beginning of another chain of events that leads someone else at some other point in time to take a particular action or make a particular plan based on what someone else had told him… and so on and so forth *ad infinitum*.

Even if we erroneously assume that the planning is in our control, what is not is the outcome of the plan. On the first trip, we could or could not have reached in time for the demonstration. We could have lost our way (which we did at first), asked around, and not have made it on time.

It is truly incredible that so many direct and indirect factors conspire in order for us to be where we find ourselves in the present moment. Could that possibly be in anyone's control?

We don't choose to breathe. Breathing happens. Similarly, life happens whether planned or unplanned. A fantastic engineering of events has led right up to this moment in which you are reading these words. Did you 'plan' to buy this book? Didn't it depend on a review you read, or a friend's suggestion, or a store you found it in? And even if you did plan to buy it, the book had to be in existence in the first place, which in turn needed to depend on an author getting inspired to write it and, thereafter, editors, publishers, paper merchants, printers, transporters, distributors, bookstores and so on – everyone playing their role, which enabled the book to come into existence and find its way into your hands. They all had to come together in the duration of time for you to fulfil your destiny of reading this now. Isn't that an awe-inspiring thought – the number of people and events who have come together to shape the destiny of what this moment has to offer?

Consciousness needs to be given not only a standing ovation but an encore for the fantastic conducting of the orchestra that delicately intersperses your life with people and events to which you respond and react, and it doesn't mind if you are taking the entire credit for it. After all, you are an aspect of the same Consciousness identified as the 'me' – as a separate body-mind intellect, busy planning your next move on the chessboard of life. But when it is realised that planning is just a mechanism for the 'me' to function in daily living, the planning is no longer stained with the stickiness of the 'me' and its projections into the future, along with all the expectations, which if not manifested would cause tremendous angst, grief, regret, guilt and all the possible 'What did I do wrong?' scenarios.

The subject of 'things not going according to plan' reminds me of a recent conversation. A few days ago there was an article in the newspapers about a local restaurant in the neighbourhood of Colaba in South Mumbai, which had been robbed at knife-point. Alongside the article was an image of a CCTV grab of the same. The robbery was caught on camera but the difficulty was that the camera, being on the ceiling, only got a top-angle shot of the action. So, one could only see the tops of the heads of the robbers and that of the cashier. This was a no-good situation and I wondered how the cops would ever be able to nab the culprits. To my surprise, in a couple of days, the newspapers announced that the robbery had been solved and the criminals arrested, thanks to the CCTV footage. The next day, I happened to meet the Deputy Commissioner of Police in the health club that we both frequent. I told him that I marvelled at how the cops busted the thieves with such little evidence. With a wry smile on his face, he shot back: "Sometimes we catch them, in spite of our best efforts." He was sardonically pointing to the fact that the police are always accused of not being competent enough even though they put in their best efforts. However, he couldn't have expressed it better for, more often than not, we plan things and put in our best, but the outcome is not always the one that we had hoped for or expected.

When it is realised that you are just a part of the

functioning of Totality, you don't take the weight of your life and the world on your shoulders. You rest in the knowing that, ultimately, a plan fructifies only if it is ordained by the will of the Source.

With this understanding that 'planned' or 'unplanned', we will be exactly where we are supposed to be at a given point in time, there arises a sense of a deep relaxation. If things don't go according to plan, it becomes much simpler to accept that they were not meant to. After all, you really didn't do the planning in the first place – too many factors contributed to making the plan. 'Events not going according to the plan' was precisely what was supposed to happen, as part of the Divine plan. Could it be that the outcome was already fixed, and for that outcome to manifest, things were not supposed to go according to your precious little plan?

Meanwhile, if things do go according to plan, we simply cannot usurp all the credit for the planning, for we know that just like a beautiful Kashmiri carpet comes together thanks to a thousand intricate weaves to present an exquisite design, similarly, a fantastic tapestry of events and people are interwoven in order to fructify 'our' plan. 'Failure' and 'success' are just labels given by the 'me' to define what the outcome of the plan is. The outcome didn't ask to be judged by a 'me'; it is a label that the 'me' stuck onto the outcome.

Viewed from this perspective, the attachment to and the involvement in the plan drops away. The plan is not taken that 'personally' anymore for the simple reason that there were too many people and factors involved in it. Does it mean one should not plan as, in any case, one would be exactly where one is supposed to be, plan or no plan? Certainly not. Planning is a mechanism of daily living. If planning happens, one lets it happen. If planning doesn't happen, one goes with the flow. We will do what is in our nature to do.

33, Belgrave Square.

I wonder when and if events will lead me there again. Do I plan to visit there again? I don't. Does it mean I won't? It doesn't.

And that's assuming the Spiritual Centre doesn't shift to another location over the years.

THE EXTREMITY OF GOD'S WILL

When I was twelve years old and my family was holidaying in Mussoorie, my mother picked up a statue of Joan of Arc from an antique shop. It was a beautiful, white porcelain statue that looked at least a couple of hundred years old. It depicted Joan tied with ropes to a stake, standing on a pile of logs, clasping a gold-painted cross to her chest. It was quite a baffling image for my young mind – why was such a young, innocent looking girl tied up like this to be burnt? What a contradiction it was. I remember wondering why someone was tied up for praying to God.

My mother told me that Joan was a saint who was considered a witch by some, and that's why she was burnt at the stake. I simply couldn't get my head around that. When I thought of her as a witch, I was afraid. When I thought of her as a saint, I was elated. Which version should I believe? So I used to love her at times and I used to fear her at other times. As I grew older, I read up more and more on Joan and it became a fascinating obsession of sorts, especially as I used to meet her every day in my living room! As I learnt more about Joan, my heart ached for the injustice that was meted out to her.

Although there are many sordid episodes in the world's history that simply don't make sense and are bereft of reason, it's hard to match that of Joan of Arc. This episode displayed the extremities of 'good' and 'bad' that human beings are capable of. The price to be paid for the remembrance of this chapter in history was the loss of an extraordinary teenager's life in a most gruesome way for what appeared to be the silliest of reasons.

Joan emerged in the midst of a dark and dreary political period in France. During the Hundred Years' War, after years of constant defeat, France was completely demoralised. There was no hope left, as all options had been exhausted. It was in this scenario that young Joan, all of sixteen, knocked on the Dauphin's door. She said she heard Divine voices instructing her to lead France to victory against the English. She asked to be placed at the head of the army in order to fulfil the Divine prophecy. After some deliberations over this preposterous suggestion, the young Dauphin agreed. For there was simply nothing to lose, and the young girl was certainly charged with a rare determination else she wouldn't have even reached this far.

Soon Joan, a peasant girl, had stunning successes on the battlefield as one victory followed another. What's more, she fulfilled her promise and managed to get the Dauphin, young Charles VII, installed as King despite the stiff opposition that he faced.

After his coronation, the battles continued. It seemed there was no stopping Joan. However, in one minor battle with the Burgundians, Joan's army was outmanoeuvred. She ordered a retreat and, in keeping with what was honourable to do, was the last to leave the field. Unfortunately, the opposing army surrounded the rear guard. Joan was forced to dismount and was taken as prisoner of war.

She was promptly sold to the English. They wanted to waste no time in getting rid of her, but they couldn't put her to death for giving them a whipping on the battlefield. So, they decided to brand her a witch and a heretic, and the Divine voices that she claimed she heard proved perfect fodder.

Joan was thus put on trial, and all stops were pulled out to ensure that it was one of the most unfair trials in history. She was chained in an iron cage and denied an advocate or any form of proper legal counsel. What's more, transcripts of her answers during the trial were altered. There was no way out. But what was most appalling was the fact that Joan was left all alone to defend herself. It would not have been a difficult task for Charles VII to sort out this situation, but he did nothing to save Joan even though she had helped coronate him King. Joan was surrounded by a vacuum of loss from all sides and hoped for at least one friendly card – which was never dealt. Throughout the trial, it was Joan's innocence that was on display for all to see. For her answers to the seasoned vultures hovering around her came as swift replies, without any deliberation on her part. She had no idea what they would ask her next, nor had she any experience or training in politics.

Joan's total acceptance of God's will

Reading Bernard Shaw's *Saint Joan** had a deep impact on me. He won the Nobel Prize for Literature and this play,

---

* *Saint Joan*, George Bernard Shaw, Penguin Classics.

an international success, was instrumental in his winning it. *Saint Joan* was one of the most objective presentations of this chapter in history, and large parts of the dialogues were based on actual recorded transcripts. Above all, in Shaw's handling of the subject I saw certain facets of the philosophy of Advaita shining through. It was clear that Shaw was a man of tremendous understanding.

Joan had the total and unequivocal belief that she was carrying out God's will. At her trial, when the Inquisitor asked Joan if she would believe the Church was wiser than her if they told her that her visions were sent by the devil to tempt her to her damnation, she replied that it was her belief that only God was wiser than her, and it was His command that she would carry out. What's more, she said that all of the actions that the Inquisitors called her 'crimes' were performed by her in accordance with God's command. She had done those things by the order of God alone. Joan's position was clear; her allegiance was with God and no authority could step in the middle to claim that it knew God's will better as far as she was concerned. After all, she had had a direct communion with God. Thus, when she was asked if the voices commanded her not to submit to the Church, she simply replied that her voices did not tell her to disobey the Church but that God must be served first.

Joan was obviously answering questions based on what she felt in her heart. She was simply following a Divine command. So you can well imagine how strange it might have seemed to her that she was being tried for heresy! How could anyone else tell her what God's will was when she knew exactly what it was.

Shaw was clearly trying to show that the Church was taking the higher ground and usurping the authority of God by questioning Joan about her relationship with God. But Joan, in her innocence, would have none of it.

Who determines God's will?

Shaw was actually laying bare the greater issue that was at stake besides the burning of Joan of Arc; the issue of religion and its institutions 'unknowingly placing themselves above the deity'.

The Church was hell-bent on proving that Joan's alleged offences were not political offences against England (that seemed a minor quibble) but, rather, against God.

Thus, the Church wanted Joan to accept its interpretation of God's will and not her own. It was a peculiar situation and an impossible task – calling on her to accept its own interpretation of God's will, and to sacrifice her own. Of course, she flatly refused. For hers was a direct experience and thus her Truth. After all, who decides God's will? Could any entity, institution or individual claim to know what God's will was for someone else? It was tantamount to telling a shadow not to follow the substance that it is a shadow of. Could a shadow do anything else but waltz with its Creator?

The dialogue persistently goes on. Joan is asked if she felt she was in God's grace. This was a lethal legal trap, for according to the Church no one could be certain of being in God's grace. If she answered yes, that would seal her fate as a heretic. She answered, without the slightest hesitation, "If I am not, may God put me there; and if I am, may God so keep me."

Where else could this trial have led? Joan's answers were stoking the coals of the inquisition, and the outcome was inevitable. In yet another display of her innocence which was perceived as arrogance, when she was asked if she, and not the Church, was supposed to be the judge in this matter, she replied: "What other judgement can I judge by but my own?"

Anyway, to cut Joan's short life story shorter, after much manipulation and bickering, she was eventually found guilty of heresy and burnt at the stake on 30th May 1431. The absurdity of it was that one of the key charges levied against her was that she dressed in male attire, a ground for heresy! It did not matter that she would have needed to if she was part of an attacking army, and also in order to be considered as one of the soldiers. She could hardly have been expected to go to battle in a frock.

Nevertheless, her demeanour at the stake was such that it moved all those who were witness to tears. She held tight a cross given to her by a peasant, and also asked for a cross to be held before her that she could see through the rising flames. She started to chant the name of Jesus until her voice could no longer be heard. Young Joan did not lose faith in her beloved God right till the very end. And that was the end of an eventful life of a girl who listened to the voices in her head, did what God willed her to do, and got roasted on the fires of an unjust judgement because of it! In our daily living, we wonder aloud and question God when things don't exactly go our way. Is it possible for us to even imagine what Joan must have felt?

Another great truth was reflected in this episode. You never know what the next moment will bring. Joan's voices could not guarantee her success the next moment on the battlefield. Nor did they save her from her fate. What's more, it's a clear example of the fact that being a good person and doing good deeds is not an insurance against anything bad happening. And why do bad things happen to good people? There is no possible answer to this question for we can never know the basis of God's will. Could you imagine being burnt at the stake for listening to God and winning wars for your country when you're only nineteen years old? Joan could hardly have dreamt that such a fate would befall her, especially when she was the recipient of a Divine command through the voices that spoke to her.

After the pyre burnt out, the English raked back the coals so what remained of her could be seen and no one could claim that Joan had escaped alive. They then burnt the remains again to reduce them to ashes and, to prevent any collection of relics, they cast them into the Seine.

However, legend has it that Joan's heart would not burn.

God's will prevails

The only consolation of this chapter in history is in knowing that the force that led her to hear the voices was the same force that led her to her death. Just as she was 'being lived' – to lead France, in defiance of all common sense – so also were those responsible for her death. Joan's life could not have got cut short unless it was, ultimately, God's will.

This episode was a perfect example of the polaric extremities of 'good' and 'bad'. That Joan was born as a peasant in a village set the perfect conditions for a simple, pure and innocent upbringing. It was with this as her foundation that she received the voices without ever questioning the validity of her experience. Nor was she deterred from approaching the young Dauphin with the strangest of requests to lead the country in war.

With her stupendous success, it was only natural that she was a symbol for the 'good', and proved to be a thorn in the flesh of the 'bad' – her detractors and the enemy camps. They obviously would do all that they could to get rid of this young pest who had consistently humiliated them on the battlefield. The whole event turned out to be a political one as far as they were concerned, and her 'voices from God' are what they used against her to brand her a witch and a heretic.

Yet, the fact remains that all the characters in this real-life drama were lived to act the way they did. This is exemplified in Shaw's play where the Bishop Cauchon tells Joan: "They will see in me evil triumphing over good, falsehood over truth, cruelty over mercy, hell over heaven. Their courage will rise as they think of you, only to faint as they think of me. Yet God is my witness I was just, I was merciful. I was faithful to my light: I could do no other than I did."

Shaw, in his sheer genius, was driving home the point to the audience that ultimately it was God's will that operated through each and every character in this event. Everyone was driven to act the way they did, seeing things from their point of view. Isn't that also what's happening today? Terrorists are carrying out barbaric acts because from their point of view, it's the right thing to do. Joan's story became a perfect exposition on human nature – the extreme possibility of 'good' as well as 'bad'. That's one reason why this story has endured and fascinated us through the ages. For its extremity has shone light on the injustice we humans can inflict on others. The situation is no different today as it was in Joan's days.

Passing such a severe judgement on her, ordering her to be burnt at the stake, was in itself the biggest travesty of justice. What's more, it was ironic that what was judged was the mechanism – the voices in her head – and not the actual outcome of her actions. For how in God's name could she have been judged for winning wars for her country? But all that is water under the bridge. Ultimately, all parties did exactly what they thought was right to do. Who is to judge whom for what? It's convenient for you and me to judge the events as they played out and side with the good, considering that it was 'right'. But if you were a tyrant, or a general in an army, wouldn't you do what you considered pragmatic and get rid of the problem in the quickest way possible? It just so happened that burning people at the stake was fashionable in those days. In this day and age a swifter mode of dispensing so-called 'justice' would have done the job.

A judgement on judgement

While actions certainly have to be judged in order to maintain law and order in society (although we can see how this could be abused), what this brings us face to face with is the issue of judgement in our everyday living. This life that we find ourselves in is the domain of separation – 'me' and the 'other'. We are constantly judging people as good or bad and right or wrong. It is how the 'me' – the identified consciousness – functions. It considers itself different from the 'other'. We consider ourselves as the 'subject' and the 'other' as the object, and pronounce judgement on the object. Little do we realise that what we consider our object considers us as its object and itself as the subject. This subject-object/object-subject play goes on and on in the dance of duality.

And what is our judgement based on? It is based on the filters of our conditioning and nature. Our judgement is based on what someone did in 'our' eyes. It is already a coloured judgement as far as the truth is concerned. What's more, we forget that the person has performed his action based on his own background and conditioning. Through these filters we view 'what is' and pronounce judgement on the same. The untainted, pure truth of who we all truly are is weighed down by these layers at both ends of the stick – subject and object. What emerges is a distortion of reality. Somebody is thus right or wrong according to our filters, which make certain things right or wrong for us. It was Jalalludin Rumi who said, "Out beyond ideas of wrong-doing and right-doing, there is a field. I will meet you there."

Perhaps this is what Jesus was pointing to when he said, "Judge not, that ye not be judged." For we are all victims of our conditioning. We can only find fault (which means passing a judgement) in others if we ourselves know what it is we accuse them of. We have to have that aspect within ourselves in order to recognise it. So when we judge others, we're truly judging ourselves.

Burning at the stake seems to be a favourite pastime even today. For whenever we pass a judgement on someone, that's exactly what we're doing. We are in the realm of duality, 'me' and 'you'. This means constantly judging people – oneself or others. Not only people, but also constantly judging situations and feelings.

Judgements start dropping away when we see that we're all shaped by our inherent nature and our upbringing. Judgements start dropping away when it is seen that it is the same energy that animates each of us, that expresses itself through the filters of six billion 'me's. Whatever happens through each one of us is ultimately the will of the Source – God – Consciousness.

I remember an incident with my ex-girlfriend. We had gone out to dinner with some friends, a couple who were married for many years. At the end of the dinner, on our way home, she remarked how blissfully happy and in love the couple seemed despite the number of years they had been married. I mentioned to her that it was interesting she felt that since, in reality, the husband was having an affair. She was shocked. How could he do such a thing to his wife? She did not want to see him ever again. Then, she trained her guns on me and asked if I had told him that what he was doing was wrong. I said that I hadn't for the simple reason that I did not know the details of his affair, nor did it interest me. What's more, he didn't even ask me whether what he was doing was wrong or right. Who was I to intervene and pass judgement? Intervention would have been meddling, and passing judgement irrelevant.

She was mortified when she heard me say this for she felt I was condoning his affair. What's more, she wondered aloud that if I was condoning his affair, I would condone myself if I had an affair if we got married. Judgement after judgement was passed, this time on me! The badge of 'ex' was pinned on my chest and she passed the final judgement that our relationship was over. In that one evening I was burnt at the stake more than a few times! Nevertheless, it is clear that she too was 'lived' to think the way she did, a thinking based on her 'filters', which determined how she viewed the world.

As can be seen, we're constantly judging ourselves as well as others. Each time a judgement is passed, we're tossing one more log onto Joan's pyre. We're constantly judging 'what is' and in turn projecting a 'what should be'.

So what does all this talk about judgement mean? Should one judge or not? The matter needs to be seen in perspective. It is the 'me' that judges – it is almost an automatic aspect of functioning in daily living. But it is seen that the 'me', like the 'other', is just an instrument through whom God's will functions. Each 'me' reacts and responds the way it is conditioned to. It is the 'me' operating in the realm of duality that judges, for it assumes that it is the 'subject' of the object that it judges. The impersonal awareness that functions through 'you', 'me', 'he' and 'she' is not concerned with judgement, as it is impersonality itself. It is the consciousness that is identified as a 'me' separate from the 'other' that judges. But, Consciousness as impersonal awareness is not concerned.

When seen from this perspective, judgement loses its grip on 'me'. Even if a judgement is passed, it is more of an automatic functioning without the usual intensity and involvement in the judging. I become less harsh in my judgements about the people and situations I find myself in.

I thus become less harsh in my judgements about myself. The fires of the impersonal awareness that I truly am, not the limited 'me and my story', burn brighter. The judgement of the 'me' is sacrificed at the stake.

There is a French saying: *"Tout comprendre, c'est tout pardonner,"* which means, "To understand all is to forgive all." To understand what? That all there is, is Consciousness, and we all are appearances in Consciousness. 'Me' and the 'other' are objects in Consciousness with their respective filters through which the world is viewed. Consciousness has identified itself with 'you', 'me', 'he' and 'she'. Nevertheless, we are Consciousness masquerading as the identified 'me' in the waking and dreaming states, and impersonal consciousness in the deep sleep state. We are That, or rather, That is us.

A friend once remarked: "We have nothing in common," to a friend who he felt had let him down. That statement struck me deeply. It is so true in this realm of separation. People are different. You get along with some and you don't get along with others. At the same time, his statement couldn't be further from the truth for we have everything in common as it is the same energy that functions through all of us. It is Consciousness that enabled him to make the statement to his friend and enabled his friend to hear what he said. Without that, nothing would have happened.

Coming back to the quotation regarding 'forgive all', Ramesh Balsekar could not have put it better when he said, "True forgiveness is forgiving yourself for wanting to forgive someone else for something they are supposed to have done." For, in the ultimate analysis, everything that happens is the Divine will in operation, whether we consider it right or wrong.

This is the field that Rumi referred to when he said, "Out beyond ideas of wrong-doing and right-doing, there is a field. I will meet you there." It is the field of Consciousness that is not tainted by 'me' and my judgements. It is the impersonal awareness of being, of Presence, that exists as 'us' before the 'me' comes marching in.

The heart of Joan

How could Joan's heart ever burn? When she knows her fate is sealed, Shaw's Joan says, "I will go out now to the common people and let the love in their eyes comfort me, for the hate in yours. You will all be glad to see me burnt; but before I go through the fire I shall go through it to their hearts for ever and ever... I shall be remembered when men will have forgotten where Rouen stood. I hope men will be the better for remembering me and they would not remember me so well if you had not burnt me."

What a tragedy. For Joan to be remembered by you and me today, she had to be burnt at the stake. What's more, she was canonised a saint only because it was recognised that a grave wrong had been done to her by branding her a heretic. For all you know, if she weren't branded a heretic, she might not have been canonised. Truth be told, she was canonised for the wrong reasons (another judgement!). For when she was declared a heretic, Charles had to make sure that the trial would be annulled. If it wasn't, then it would have meant that he was assisted in his coronation by a heretic, and it would have put his kingship at stake! What a twisted fate history weaves. Can you imagine the twists and turns time had to take in order for you to be where you are today?

Now, all the characters in that real life drama are dead and gone, and only live in us as a memory and the feeling the memory evokes – a feeling that arises in our hearts. Saint Joan lives on in us, for we identify with her pain each time a judgement is passed. The heart of Joan could never be burnt for she still lives in our hearts. This point was driven home to me like clanging church bells when an acquaintance, in reference to what he overheard being said about him in a condescending way, mentioned, "In that instance, I felt like Joan of Arc!"

In Shaw's play the executioner says, "She is more alive. Her heart would not burn, nor drown. I was a master at my craft, but I could not kill the Maid. She is up and alive everywhere."

NOTHING SHORT OF A MIRACLE!

One morning, a taxi driver came to Ramesh's talk. He said to Ramesh: *"Maine suna ki aap sant hein, to mein help ke liye aaya hoon"* (I heard that you are a sage, so I have come to you for help). He then went on to narrate that he had come to Mumbai forty years ago, and had been driving a taxi for a living. However, his life hadn't improved over the years. He always had hopes that he would do better, but nothing came of it. Many years had rolled by. When he heard of Ramesh he thought he would come meet him and get some help from this modern sage. He said, "What shall I do, how shall I improve my situation? I have kept hoping and trying… I got married, had children, they grew up, and yet here I am… still a taxi driver! Still trying to make a living. Still struggling to make ends meet. So tell me, what shall I do?"

After a very brief pause, Ramesh replied, "It's simple. Get used to the idea!"

The taxi driver was taken aback. Is that all he would get from the sage? He did not take this advice kindly. He replied, "I come to you for help, and this is what you tell me? This is all you have to say? What kind of a sage are you?" And Ramesh said, "But don't you see… I *am* helping you. You yourself have said that you have been trying to improve your situation all these years, but in spite of your best efforts nothing much has come of it. So, accept the situation and the fact that this was your destiny."

But the taxi driver was hoping for a miracle and he felt like he had landed up at the wrong place for that. Or, had he? Perhaps this was what he needed to hear, something as simple as being told that it's better to accept 'what is'. After all, it's not like he had come to Mumbai just a couple of years ago and then landed up at Ramesh's home. He was probably at the end of his productive years and still struggling with the fact that he had not 'made it'. Ramesh might just have given him a glimpse of the greatest miracle of all – the total acceptance of 'what is'.

But for the miracle he was looking for, he would have done better to practise the law of attraction instead of visiting Ramesh.

So much has been written on the law of attraction that in this world of duality, it's only fair to give due credit to its counterpart. I mentioned this in casual conversation to a friend. "With all this 'law of attraction' material all around... why don't we formulate a law to balance things out?" She asked me, "What would you call it?" "That's simple," I replied, in a lighter vein, "the law of distraction." It's really quite a simple law; nothing need be 'done' to implement it. Anything that takes you away from 'what is' is the law of distraction in operation. A thought may arise, but when it gets extended in the duration of thinking, then that is the law of distraction in operation. Thinking itself is not the problem, especially when it is required for planning a task at hand or even planning for the future. Ramesh used to refer to this as the 'working mind' in operation. He had this unique concept of the 'working mind' and the 'thinking mind'. The working mind operates in the present, whereas the thinking mind goes into the dead past or projects into an imaginary future. For example, when a surgeon is performing an operation and is focusing on the task at hand, it is the working mind in operation. However, if the patient is a very important person, a celebrity or politician, and the surgeon starts worrying about the consequences if something were to go wrong with the operation, then it is the thinking mind in operation. This sort of thinking would detract from the task at hand.

The rampant thinking mind has become a modern-day epidemic with too many thoughts being extended into thinking in 'horizontal time', like the tentacles of an octopus protruding from our heads. Little wonder that to 'be present' is considered something much sought after in this day and age, and it is deemed miraculous if one is able to sustain it in the midst of all the challenges of an ordinary day.

On a lighter note, the subject of miracles reminds me of a joke that someone forwarded me on the internet:

In a small town in India, a man decided to open a bar just opposite the local temple. The temple and its congregation started a petition campaign to block the bar from opening and prayed daily that his business venture would fail. Candlelight vigils and mass prayer meetings took place outside the temple every day.

Nevertheless, work progressed. However, when it was almost complete and the bar was about to open a few days later, a lightning bolt struck the bar in the middle of the night and it was burnt to the ground. Nothing remained but smoky rubble.

The temple folk were elated. Their prayers were answered. They said it was a Divine miracle. They were feeling rather smug about it. That is, until the bar owner sued the temple authorities on the grounds that the temple, through its congregation and prayers, was ultimately responsible for the destruction of his bar, either through direct or indirect actions or means.

In its reply to the court, the temple vehemently denied all responsibility or any connection that their prayers caused the bar's destruction.

After the hearing, the judge looked over the paperwork, scratched his chin and commented:

"I don't know how I'm going to decide this case, but it appears from the paperwork that we have a bar owner who believes in the power of prayer, and we have an entire temple and its devotees that don't!"

How quickly we change our position to suit our convenience. Despite all our 'thinking' and best laid plans, life takes its own twists and turns. Just the other day, a close friend was mentioning how, when his business was not doing well, he decided to wind it up. However, it simply didn't happen. For some operational reason or another, it kept chugging along. Documentation needed to be completed; government authorities had to be notified; book entries needed to be passed… various obstacles cropped up. The months dragged on until, very suddenly, the business started booming. Orders started flowing in, and the company soon became cash rich. The realisation dawned on him that in spite of his best efforts to close it, it did not happen. And if it had, then it would have been disastrous for him. It was Divine intervention that prevented him from closing down the business. And he said to me, "Truly, there is so little in our control. Now I know it through first-hand experience. If I had my way, I would have been on the streets by now!" He was fortunate that it was his destiny that his story had a happy ending... at least for the moment.

The total acceptance that one can never know what the next moment brings, pleasure or pain, is the greatest miracle. René Magritte, a leading Belgian surrealist, had produced a series of paintings on a specific theme that was titled *The Dominion of Light*. At first glance, they look like simple paintings of a house with some trees around it and the sky above. But if one looks closer, one realises that Magritte has painted a bright daylight sky, but the house and trees are painted in a night setting, with darkness and shadows. Magritte once said, "I have always had the greatest interest in the night and day, but without ever feeling any preference for one or the other."* The enlightened masters of Advaita would have cheered on hearing that, knowing they had a brother in their midst. Night and day are metaphors for pleasure and pain... sometimes what is a pleasure today turns into a sorrow tomorrow. What Magritte possibly meant was that they, being transitory in nature, no longer held sway over him.

One day, a friend was describing a sculpture which looked like a beautiful, shimmering, metallic butterfly from afar, with its motorised wings gliding gently. However, as one approaches it one is taken aback, for the wings are

* *Magritte, in the Royal Museums of Fine Arts of Belgium, Brussels,* Gisele Ollinger-Zinque.

made up of hundreds of razor blades stacked very neatly together. Suddenly, the wings of this beautiful, gentle, light and happy creation of God transform into lethal instruments of all that cuts, severs, wounds, and maims – an echo of pleasure turning into pain. No wonder the work of art is titled *Virtually Untouchable**.

When the light of understanding shines forth on the transitory nature of our experiences in daily living, acceptance of 'what is' is the natural outcome. Then, even when we're involved in incessant thinking, there is a total acceptance of the involvement without wanting it to be any other way. For, not wanting to be involved is a further involvement in the involvement, and becomes yet another venomous serpent hissing atop Medusa's head. What is needed is the single, swift stroke of the 'sword of understanding' to sever Medusa's head completely. But, by getting involved in the involvement, we're instead jabbing away at the hundreds of snakes of the thinking mind with a small penknife, hoping to kill all of them one by one.

On the subject of light, according to *Surya Vijnan* (solar science), there are 360 rays of the sun, which radiate outwards to form the creation of the entire universe. The yogi-saint Vishuddhanand Paramahansadeva** could create gemstones, sweets, and medicines by focusing the rays of the sun with the aid of a magnifying glass. Different combinations of rays could produce different objects. This means that all objects, animate or inanimate, are nothing but congealed light. So, if you're arguing with

---

* Virtually Untouchable, artist: Sunil Gawde.

** *Yogirajadhiraj Swami Vishuddhanand Paramahansadeva – Life & Philosophy*, Nand Lal Gupta, Vishwavidyalaya Prakashan, Varanasi.

someone, fighting with someone, or hating someone with all of your being, you're actually doing it with a mass of congealed light!

In my younger days, I remember staring at the sun and wondering whether it was really an object in the sky I was looking at, or whether it was actually a perfect circular hole punched into the sky through which this bright orange colour shone forth. If no one had told me, I would have never known. Perhaps God had created just a bit of an opening in the blue, or else the liquid, bright honey-gold now contained in that circle would be too strong for our eyes if the entire sky was made up of it.

It is fascinating how some concepts stay with you over the years. Some days back, I was looking at the sun through the large picture window in my office. Being on the 17th floor, we have a splendid view of the Arabian Sea. The sun looked like a dot in the vastness of the sky, and in my mind the image arose of hundreds of suns sticking together like buttons to cover the vast blue expanse. The sun is huge in itself, but how enormous must the space around it be when most of what one sees is just space. But then, there is something bigger than that as well. As Siddharameshwar Maharaj said, "The sun is millions of years away from the earth. It is also by size many times larger... We see it so small. It would take years to see it up close. From this example, you can imagine how vast and great you yourself are. The Self is very vast... the Self is so vast that as soon as you open your eyes, it does not take more than an instant to see the Sun."*

---

* *Master of Self-Realization*, Sri Siddharameshwar Maharaj, Sri Sadguru Trust.

The total acceptance of 'what is' manifests as stillness of the thinking mind. This is what is meant by the words 'be still'.

King Bimbisara of Magadha had a peculiar problem on hand. All trade was drying up in his kingdom, for the main trade route passed through dense forest in which lived a desperado who slaughtered people before stealing their goods. He was none other than the dreaded Angulimala (finger necklace). He had earned the nickname because of his peculiar habit of stringing his victims' fingers to form a garland that he wore around his neck. The king sent his army to deal with this terror but Angulimala, like a force of unstoppable wrath, routed it.

The king, helpless in this predicament, then approached the Buddha. Angulimala was once such a genius, an intellectual prodigy, that he became a threat to his own guru. Jealous of his abilities, the guru engineered for him to be disgraced and banished from the ashram. In those days, this was as good as death and the young man's mind snapped and he became a bandit. But the Buddha felt he could still salvage this great soul. On sighting the Buddha walking in the forest one day, Angulimala gave chase but no matter how hard he tried, the serene monk outpaced him. He simply couldn't figure out how! Exhausted, and at his wit's end, he shouted, "Stand still, oh monk!" The Buddha replied, "I am still. Be thou still also." Angulimala's mental constructs came crashing down at that very moment. He knew the Buddha was referring to mental and emotional stillness, and he realised he was in the presence of a greater and stronger being than his violent and vengeful self.*

---

* *The Sacred India Tarot,* Rohit Arya and Jane Adams, Yogi Impressions.

One day, I was sitting on the floor opposite a big mirror. The mirror was actually placed on the twin doors of the cupboard. Hence, it was split vertically down the middle, with a small gap of a centimetre separating the left and right sides. On that day, the cupboard was slightly ajar by a couple of inches. When I looked into the mirror, I could see beautiful green trees reflected – that was the view outside the window that was across the mirror. There was a sacred stillness in this reflection – it seemed other-worldly. Then I realised why this was so. It wasn't that it was just a beautiful reflection. What I realised was that 'I' was missing from the reflection. The two doors being slightly ajar had created a kind of optical illusion in which I, who was seated right in the middle, disappeared from the reflection. Everything directly above and below me did too, but the rest of the surrounding was intact.

Things look so much more serene and calm when there is no 'me' looking at them. A fixed point of seeing was no longer being reflected, and there was a liberating feeling to seeing everything else being reflected without the body being part of it.

What immediately came up was what Nisargadatta Maharaj said: "Let me gladden your hearts by giving you a couple of tips. In spite of whatever I say, I know you will continue on your 'self-improvement' course and keep looking for tips…

a) Make it a habit to think and speak in the passive tense. Instead of "I see something" or "I hear something," why not think in the passive way: "Something is seen" or "Something is heard?" The perception will then not be on the basis of an action by the phenomenal entity but on the basis of an event or occurrence. In due course, the pseudo-entity 'I' will recede into the background.

b) Before going to sleep at night, spend about ten minutes sitting relaxed both in body and mind, taking your stand that 'you' are not the body-mind construct but the animating consciousness so this idea will impregnate your being throughout the period of your sleep."*

Some very practical advice from Maharaj, indeed.

"Be still and know that I am God," said Jesus. The Buddha would have approved. Jesus did not say, 'become still' but, rather, "be still." 'Become' would imply that one needed to become something other than what one already is, whereas stillness is our very nature. The stillness of deep sleep is also present in the waking state. In deep sleep there is impersonal consciousness, whereas in the waking state it is identified consciousness. Either way, the bedrock is Consciousness, impersonal or identified.

The same consciousness that is impersonal in deep sleep (you exist but don't know that you exist) is now identified with a name and form as a separate entity in the waking state (I am Gautam). This would, in effect, mean that even when you aren't still, in the course of the day with all the various activities going on, you actually are! The peace of deep sleep is prevalent in the waking state, even while your thinking mind is doing cartwheels as it rides horses that have bolted from the stables as swiftly as bats out of hell, galloping into the dead past or an imaginary future, and a fantasy world of innumerable 'what ifs', while riding away from the greatest miracle of all – 'what is'.

---

* *Pointers from Nisargadatta Maharaj*, Ramesh Balsekar, Chetana.

And finally, Ramana Maharshi quoting the words of Jesus '...Be still and know that I am God', elaborated on them by adding, "To be still is not to think. Know, and not think, is the word."*

Be still, and know THAT I am God. The Source. Consciousness – impersonal or identified.

---

* *Talks with Sri Ramana Maharshi*, Sri Munagala Venkataramiah, Sri Ramanasramam.

AWAKENING FROM THE DREAM

When I had just begun visiting Ramesh Balsekar, I remember that one of the first questions he asked was, "What do you want most in life?" I started to think about that as nobody had asked me this before. Seeing that I was taking my time to answer the question, he said, "Do you want Enlightenment? Self-realisation?" I had no idea what he was talking about. I hadn't heard those words before and didn't know what they meant. He must have seen me looking clueless sitting on the chair across him. He then went on to say, "What one wants most in life, whether one knows it or not, is peace of mind."

During his talks, he would invariably launch into his concept that peace of mind could only be had if there was the total understanding that nobody 'does' anything; everything is a happening that happens according to the will of God; and, through whom a particular happening happens is irrelevant for we are just instruments through whom God's will functions. He would lucidly lay out the various aspects of his teaching, taking a person step-by-step through it. At the end of it, he would say that one couldn't *do* anything to have peace of mind, simply because one is not the 'doer' of one's actions. This was the catch, so to speak. The total understanding, leading to peace of mind, could happen only if it was God's will. He would also say that the final understanding is that there is no 'I' to understand anything.

I used to wonder what this all meant. Eight years after I met Ramesh, my second book was published. I remember going to him with the manuscript. It was based on his essay titled *The Purpose of Life*, which he had given me to read. I asked him if he would like to read the manuscript. He said he would be delighted. When he returned it I was pleasantly surprised to see that he had written a Foreword. However, what surprised me even more was when, while reading it, I saw he had written that he knew 'awakening had taken place' for me. I wondered what this meant. I remember telling my mother that while Ramesh mentioned that according to him 'awakening had happened', how was I supposed to know? Her reply, astonishingly close to Ramesh's teaching, was, "But how could you know? Awakening doesn't happen to a 'you'."

Anyway, that was the end of it and the matter rested there. *Status quo.* Until one night, I had a dream. This dream gave me a much clearer understanding of what all this meant.

In the dream, I was calling up a friend. At the same time, I saw my friend receiving the call. This was peculiar. It was like a movie, in which you see that the screen splits in two, on the left is the caller talking into the phone and on the right is the receiver of the call listening and answering back. Only, in the dream this split screen wasn't there. Don't ask me how, but both the scenes were playing out simultaneously.

It struck me (in the dream) that if I could see myself calling and also see my friend receiving the call at the same time, then surely I was separate from myself – the caller. And, of course, I was not the receiver of the call. So, if I was not the caller and nor was I the receiver, then who was I? It was clear that I was a witness who witnessed this event happening. I was the ground upon which this event of the call being made by me and being received by another was happening. It was so clear – I was not me – the caller, but I was something impersonal in which this whole event occurred. However, stating this does not feel entirely correct. Rather, there was something impersonal in which the event took place, and there was the awareness of that impersonality as well. How peculiar – this entire process of rationalisation was taking place in the dream.

And then... I woke up!

Upon waking, the entire scene disappeared with the dream. It vanished. There was no caller and no receiver of the call. More importantly, there was no dreamer dreaming a dream. However, the dream was still vividly clear to me. The chips fell into place, enabling me to understand this whole business of awakening. For I did not 'choose' to wake up from the dream.

That which woke up was outside the dream – outside the time and space of the dream. There was no conscious decision to wake up from the dream. You don't tell yourself in a dream, "Ok, now I have had enough of dreaming and I will wake up." Waking up 'happened'. You do not decide when to end the dream. When the dream ends, the characters in the dream disappear. Upon waking, the dream was seen for what it was – simply a dream. And the characters in the dream were illusory, for they disappeared along with the dream. Everything was such a brilliant piece of fiction, the only truth being that one is awake – here and now!

Then the memory of my teacher's favourite quotation, one he would often repeat during his last months, came to mind. This was from Adi Sankara's *Viveka-chudamani* (The Crest-Jewel of Discrimination), "The world that you see in your dream is a projection of the mind. The world in the waking state is also a projection of the same mind." He then went on to explain that one's dream world is therefore as real or unreal as this world we appear to live in. He said, "When I remember that the world I see now is no different from my dream world, then I know all that I need to know! I do not care a damn about my dream world, so why should I care about this one?"

In the living dream of life, 'awakening' means the total seeing that all the characters in this living dream are illusory, including 'me'. Yet, the 'you' and 'me' are functional aspects of the living dream. The characters are simply playing out their roles in the dream of living, and the ground on which the roles are being played out is nothing but Consciousness. Without Consciousness, there can be no characters; no 'you', 'me', 'he' and 'she'... Consciousness is the content of everything in the living dream. It is important to understand that awakening cannot happen to a character in this living dream, it cannot happen to a 'you' in the living dream of life. In a dream, it is not the character in the dream who wakes up. The 'you' cannot turn around and say, "I am awakened" simply because it cannot be... for it is a character in the living dream. Rather, the 'you' that you thought you were is seen as an illusion from that space which is not the 'you' or the 'other' – from the ground of impersonal awareness. The impersonal awareness is present all along; it is also present as the dreamer of the dream in which the dreamed characters appear.

Therefore, it is clear that Consciousness is identified consciousness when it has identified itself with a character in the living dream of life (me and my story) with a particular body. But even so, it is not separate from that which we truly are – impersonal awareness.

To reiterate, how can you possibly see the 'you' that is the character in the living dream, while you are still the character in the living dream? It's like the character in a movie seeing that he is an actor in a role, while he is acting out the role. It's impossible – he *is* the role while it is being acted out! The identification is seen from the ground of impersonality, from that which is not 'you'. The actor in the role knows that he is acting out a role and that is not his true identity, for he is that which is prior to the role of the character, which he still is even while acting out the role, and what he will still be after the role is over. He does not lose who he actually is when he is acting out the role. He knows who he really is.

There is truly no 'you' to be awakened. All there is is this 'awakeness' in which there is a total seeing that all the pleasures and pains of life are faced by a 'me' that is identified consciousness, a character in the living dream; but what 'one truly is' is the impersonal awareness that witnesses this. This awakeness is one's true nature, for without this there would be no dreamer and therefore no dreamed characters. In other words, 'This' is everyone's true nature. How could there be anything special about being awake?

Consciousness is all there is – whether identified as a dreamed character, or as impersonal awareness. It is That in which the dreamer dreaming a dream pops up, and into which the dreamer dreaming the dream disappears. But all along, it is the same Consciousness – the characters and the dreamer and That which is awake are its aspects.

The next time you wake up, ask yourself... "Who woke up?"

THE DOOR TO PARADISE

Nisargadatta Maharaj was not in favour of having a samadhi in his memory once he passed away. It would have been ironic if he had been, for his entire teaching revolved around the concept that 'you are not your body'. Maharaj would often say, "You are not your body-mind. As long as you identify yourself with the body-mind, you are vulnerable to sorrow and suffering." His position was that we are not bodies that have consciousness but it is Consciousness that manifests in and as different bodies. When visitors came to ask questions, he would tell them not to pose the questions from one individual to another, but from consciousness to consciousness. "I speak to consciousness and not to an individual." This is why he would encourage seekers to read the Bhagavad Gita from the standpoint of Krishna – impersonal consciousness, and not Arjuna – identified consciousness.

A few years ago, I visited S. Mullarpattan's home in South Mumbai. He had been Maharaj's translator for several years. At that first meeting, I asked Mullarpattan if there were still any unpublished talks of Maharaj. Surely there must be tapes of many recordings. If so, it would be wonderful to bring them out as a book. He was skeptical.

It was the first time we had met. He said, "What's the point? Aren't enough talks published? All Maharaj says is to 'abide in your Beingness'." "Fair enough," I said. It was a valid point. However, I kept the offer open as I thought it would be useful to publish any of Maharaj's yet unpublished transcripts for the benefit of anyone interested in the teaching. One never knows what clicks where and when, and with whom. A word here, a sentence there... and a profound shift could take place in a reader. As far as I was concerned, even if I was not donning the hat of a practical publisher, I would still consider it a worthy effort even if it impacted just one person.

The next time I visited Mullarpattan, he asked me, "Tell me one sentence of Maharaj's that appealed to you, and tell me quickly now – don't *think* about it. Choose just one sentence from all you have read and know about Maharaj." I immediately blurted out, "Only the dead can die." He looked at me for a few seconds and then, pointing to a dusty box lying on a ledge above the door, asked me to bring it down. I did so. He said that it contained ten tapes of unpublished talks and that they were mine to bring out as a book if I wished to. It was these ten tapes that later took the form of the book *Beyond Freedom – Talks with Sri Nisargadatta Maharaj*. I heaved a sigh of relief when I read in the transcripts of one of the talks, that Maharaj said: "I am speaking differently today. As a matter of fact, this should also have been published as it is in greater detail, and is emphasising different aspects."

Only the dead can die, not the living. When I first read that sentence, I loved it. It hit me straight in the heart. I had no clue what it meant nor did I want to know.

Yet, I knew that it was the deepest truth despite the apparent absurdity of the statement. That's what I loved about it – *prima facie* it made no sense to the mind. That was Maharaj – he would pack powerful punches with his one-liners. And, if he is talking as consciousness to consciousness and not as one individual to another, then *who* cares whether one understands such a statement? It was such fun to read Maharaj.

What did Maharaj mean by 'abide in your Beingness', as Mullarpattan mentioned? In his words, "When everything else has been changing, what has not changed is the constant sense of presence, the sense you exist, the sense – I am." Abide in this 'I am', is what he meant. In other words, not 'I am Gautam', but simply Conscious Presence – 'I am'. We are this Conscious Presence and not our body – which is merely an object through which Consciousness functions. We are not the identified consciousness that we think we are – identified with a name and form as a separate person, separate from others – rather we are the impersonal 'I am'. Ramesh would give an apt description to explain the 'I am': "If all your memory were wiped out, what you would be left with is the impersonal awareness of being – 'I am'."

I did not have the good fortune to meet Maharaj, but I was blessed to have met and spent a number of years with his disciple Ramesh Balsekar who in turn became a renowned teacher. The first few books Ramesh wrote were a tribute to Maharaj's teaching. However, Ramesh realised that although there were many seekers who were deeply impacted by Maharaj's teaching, there were also some who could not 'get' what Maharaj said. The reason for this was clear: although Maharaj used to say that he was talking as consciousness to consciousness, the fact remained that whatever questions people had concerned themselves as separate individuals. While Maharaj consistently pointed back to the 'I am', there were those who were so identified with 'me and my story' that they simply did not find solace in Maharaj's words. The fact is that in the waking state, it is the identified consciousness – identified with a name and form as a separate entity – that is functioning. For some egos, being told not to ask questions as an individual was a bit hard to digest. After all, the ego *is* the separate individual. The 'leap of faith' Maharaj was asking for could just not be taken by them, for the mind and intellect simply could not let go of this identification.

This is where Ramesh's teaching helped resolve the dilemma for some of those seekers. Ramesh's conditioning – being a banker for thirty-seven years – helped him present his concepts, based on Maharaj's teaching, in a pragmatic, step-by-step manner, for the benefit of the 'individual' sitting before him. Ramesh was clear that there was no escaping the fact that he was talking to the 'ego', identified with a name and form as a separate body, in the waking state. He was not talking to the impersonal consciousness prevalent in the deep sleep state (when you exist, but you don't know that you exist), nor was he talking to the 'I am' – impersonal awareness of being, identified with a separate body but not as an 'individual'. He was clearly talking to the ego, 'I am Gautam'.

So, the crux of the matter was, how could one bring the identified consciousness as close as possible to the peace of the impersonal consciousness (figuratively speaking) that is the peace of deep sleep, in the waking state? In the waking state, it is the mind of the individual that is not at peace. How could one bring the 'me', the ego, the individual, as close as possible to impersonal functioning in the waking state, to taste this peace? The doorway to this impersonal functioning, according to Maharaj, would have to be through the impersonal awareness of being – 'I am'.

Ramesh was very clear that it was not the ego that had to be killed, for the simple reason that the ego is the functional element in the waking state, and as such is obviously necessary for 'living' to happen. Instead, it is the sense of 'doership' in the ego that needs to be uprooted. And, how is this sense of 'doership' to be uprooted? With the total understanding that all actions are Divine happenings that have to happen exactly as they do, and we are just instruments through whom the same energy that produces those very happenings – Consciousness – functions. It is the same energy that functions through each of us, just like electricity functions through each gadget in the kitchen. When there is the total understanding that nobody truly 'does' anything – as we are all 'programmed' by our genes and conditioning, and have no control over either – then there is the realisation that everything is a happening that had to happen based on the will of the Source – which some refer to as God. If this understanding is prevalent, then pleasure may arise but not pride or arrogance (not 'my' action), and regret may arise but not guilt or shame (not 'my' action either). Absence of pride, arrogance, guilt or shame, is peace of mind.

This is of course an over-simplification of Ramesh's as well as Maharaj's teachings. There are ample books on the same, and nothing more needs to be added to them. This piece of writing emerged to correlate the two. It was the result of a memory that came up when, many years ago, a Buddhist monk visited Ramesh and said he found his teaching didactic and different as compared to Maharaj's. I knew what he meant but I did not share his view. How could anyone whose teaching was that 'nobody does anything', or who said, 'the seeing is the only doing necessary', be didactic? For me, what Ramesh said was not even an extension of Maharaj's teaching – it was the same teaching put into different words and from a different perspective. What yoked the teachings together was – 'I am'.

While the tenet of Maharaj's teaching was 'you are That', Ramesh's was 'That is you'. There is a subtle difference though. Maharaj was talking to That and not the individual (consciousness to consciousness). Ramesh was talking to 'you' the individual, as a separate person. Either way, the 'me' was in trouble. Maharaj simply bypassed it. And Ramesh, by removing the sense of 'doership' in the 'me', brought it as close to impersonal functioning in the waking state as it could come. The combination of Maharaj's and Ramesh's teaching is like a fantastic *jugalbandi** in which the 'me', identified as a separate entity, fades into oblivion.

During Ramesh's talks, some seekers familiar with Maharaj's teaching would come and ask questions, citing sentences that Maharaj had uttered. They were not open to what was being said in the moment as they had brought along their conceptual baggage from their idea of Maharaj's

* Literally: 'entwined twins' – a type of duet performance in Indian Classical music, in which the musicians play together on different instruments.

teaching with them. The irony was that this was exactly what Maharaj used to caution seekers against! Ramesh would tell them: "Forget about what Maharaj said, you are here now... why don't we discuss what I am saying?" Of course, he did not mean any disrespect to Maharaj. He was simply responding to the need to break through the hardened wall of an intellectual understanding of Maharaj's teaching that had imprisoned the seeker within its walls. It is little wonder that Maharaj specifically told Ramesh that when he taught, he would not just parrot his words.

It needs to be clearly understood that while there is a subtle difference between the two approaches, it lies only in terms of presentation of the teaching. In effect, there is no difference between them. Why? Simply because, there is no 'difference' as such between the 'I am' (impersonal awareness of being) and the 'me' (identified consciousness). The 'me' is the 'I am' with the veil of identification as a separate 'doer' over it. This means that all the time the 'me and my story' is going on in the waking state, the 'I am' is ever-present as the witness to it. You cannot only function as a 'me' without the 'I am' – how could 'you' be conscious without any awareness of existing in the first place?

All there is, is Consciousness. In deep sleep, it is impersonal consciousness, in the waking state it is the identified consciousness. This identified consciousness is actually the impersonal awareness of being – 'I am' – though now identified with a separate being – 'Gautam'. They are different only in terms of 'states', so to speak.

The impersonal consciousness prevalent in the deep sleep state does not disappear upon waking up. Rather, in the waking state (as well as in the dreaming state) identification is super-imposed upon it. They are not separate and hence, do not exist independently of each other. This means that the peace of deep sleep is inherently prevalent in the waking state – it's just that the tent of the 'me' filled with hopes, desires, frustrations, anticipations and so on, has been pitched on this ground of peace. Ramana Maharshi used to say, "Deep sleep is your natural state."

To abide in the 'I am', the ego need not be killed or removed, for you are already that 'I am', which does not and cannot go anywhere. As Ramesh would say, "Who is being told to kill the ego? It is the ego that is being told to kill itself. How could the ego ever agree to this?"

However, what covers the 'I am' is the involvement in 'me and my story'. The more the involvement and the 'doership', the further away one is from the 'I am', though in truth, there is no distance between the two. *I am that I am.* This is the leap of faith. The only point is, there is no distance to leap! All 'you' need for this leap of faith is to *be* still – abide in your Beingness. *Be still and know that I am God.*

The 'I am' is the door to the peace of deep sleep in the waking state. For in the waking state you know that you exist – 'I am'. The 'I am' is That which is prior to the 'me' and what happens to it in the waking state. 'Prior' is just a pointer – there being no linear duration in time between the two. Before anything can happen to 'me', something has to be there for the happening to take place in. That something is the 'I am'. The 'me' is what gets involved in the happening, the 'I am' is That which witnesses it.

Near Srinagar, in Kashmir, is the animal sanctuary of

Dachigam. It is a thick, dense forest wherein wild animals abound. In the heart of Dachigam is a spot known as *Jannat ka Darwaza* (Door to Paradise). When you stand there, it is believed that something 'happens' to you. A friend of mine narrated to me how he had goose pimples when he stood there, and could not put his finger on why he felt so. Perhaps it was the vista of nature that was awe-inspiring, but there was something overwhelming about it. He told me, "I have never felt anything like it before. You simply must go! Words simply cannot describe it." Some locals believe that it could be the smell of the musk in the forest that heightens the senses as a result of which everything appears magical – especially at this spot, for some reason. Either way, the important point is that the Door to Paradise has no door. You simply have to stand in this spot and you are in *Jannat* (Paradise).

The 'I am' is the door to paradise, to the most supreme paradise – peace. And you're already standing at the door. Just stay at it – don't keep walking away. The 'I am' is already where you are, or rather, *who* you are in your true essence. You are not the 'me' to whom things happen but the impersonal awareness of being – 'I am' – that is the space in which things happen to the 'me'. 'I am' had to be there first, in order for 'Gautam' to be added to it. It is 'Gautam' the individual, who is trying to steer his little chariot through life, thinking he holds the reins to the horses of pleasure and pain that are drawing his chariot forward. 'Gautam' has lost sight of the fact that were it not for the simple fact that he existed – 'I am' – there would be no 'Gautam', no horses and certainly no chariot. *Read the Bhagavad Gita from the point of view of Krishna and not Arjuna.*

Conscious Presence – 'I am' – is the door to peace. Which means, the paradise of peace is Here Now, because you *are*. Peace is your natural state. Maharaj said, "The door that locks you in is the door that lets you out. The 'I am' is the door. Stay at it till it opens."

I remember a scene from a movie in which people are looking for a treasure and have a map that they are consulting. They are looking hard for the 'X' on the map that marks the spot where the treasure is buried. They had scanned the entire region high and low, but it was nowhere to be found. It was only when one of them was looking down at the floor in a pensive mood, scratching his chin, wondering where the treasure could be, that he realised that he was literally staring at an X that was on the floor slab. X indeed marked the spot, but little had they realised that it literally marked the spot on which they were standing… it was not merely a pointer to a location, it was the location!

You are not standing over the 'I am', you *are* the 'I am'. It's not that X marks the spot and you are standing over it, but you are the X! Could it possibly be any closer? There is no treasure to be found, simply because you are the treasure. Or more accurately, the treasure is you.

The cross is a brilliant symbol of the Conscious Presence. The line of horizontal time (past and future, what was, what should be, 'I am Gautam') is intersected by the line of vertical time (now, what is, 'I am'). Is the vertical line of the cross separate from the horizontal at the point at which they intersect? Does that point belong to the horizontal line or the vertical line? Ponder that. The Rosicrucians placed a white rose at this point, symbolising the flowering of Consciousness. What an apt symbol to place at this intersection.

The 'me' needn't *do* anything to be the 'I am', for it is already the 'I am'. *The seeing is the only doing necessary.* Could it get any easier? Or, could it get any tougher? It depends from which perspective it is looked at: Krishna Consciousness or identified consciousness.

Whenever I used to visit Mullarpattan, he would pull out a peacock feather. This would be a ritual at each visit. At first, I put it down to an absent mind (considering he was ninety-two) and that people often tend to repeat themselves at that age. It soon became etched in my memory like a carving in a rock-temple. He would then point to the heart of the feather, which actually looked like a heart – a deep, inky blue heart. He would then say, "That is the Beingness. And all these strands of the feather, all these other shades and colours, take you away from the Beingness." It is interesting to note that the embryological heart actually forms above the head and then later folds into the chest. In fact, our unique human face gets formed by this very separation that occurs between head and heart in our first weeks of life.

No wonder Krishna wore the feather on his head – what a perfect symbol of Krishna Consciousness. Krishna wore his heart on his head, or rather, over his head! I was pleasantly surprised to discover that the word *hriday* (heart) comes from the Sanskrit *hrudayam,* which translates as – the 'I am' dwelling in the spiritual heart.

Coming back to the 'leap of faith', it takes a certain innocence of the intellect to grasp the matter at hand. Mere mental gymnastics would get one mired in concept after concept. In order to cross over, the leap of faith is to know that there is no bridge to be built between the 'me' and the 'I am'. Nothing need be 'done' for they are not different. I am reminded of the times Ramesh would say: "What do I have to *do* to have the total understanding that I am not the 'doer'? The answer is, obviously, *nothing*!"

The innocence of the intellect is best reflected in the mind of a child. My godson Rayan, all of four years, asked his mother: "Ma, what happens to your lap when you get up?"

Answer that, and you will find a glow around you that is emanating from the embers of a bridge burning down – a bridge that never did exist in the first place.

NOTHING AND THE CENTAUR

The centaur had been my childhood companion. He was present throughout those years. He was huge, gigantic actually, perhaps more than thirty feet high. His skin was a shimmering, ethereal blue. He used to watch over me every night, while I slept in my bed by the window. I just had to open my eyes and there he would be, suspended high up in the sky. From that vantage point, he was the king of all that he surveyed. Every night, before going to sleep, I would look up at him, fascinated by this majestic creature who appeared to be striding across the starry night sky. I rested in the comfort of knowing that he was always there while I slept.

The centaur was no fantasy; he was my reality.

My centaur was unique; although his stance was one of full gallop, he stayed fixed in this one spot. Even though he roamed the galaxies, he never left his place in the sky, outside my window. He just stood poised – slowly rotating 360 degrees in one place. I would watch him turn round and round, in slow motion. He was like the earth rotating on its axis – we know that it spins at a tremendous speed but no one can sense its movement.

The centaur was a paradox. On one hand, he looked calm, composed, elegant, and above all the travails of what transpired below. He was a picture of stillness. On the other hand, his pose suggested break-neck speed as he hurtled ahead in full gallop, with his bow drawn tight and ready to shoot the arrow. *'What was he aiming at?'* I used to wonder. Whether he was facing north, south, east or west, it seemed he was perpetually aiming at nothing and that too, with such fixed attention.

One day, quite suddenly, he was taken down. His reign was over. It took an army of men to bring him down. They hacked away at his body, piece by piece, until nothing remained of him. All there remains now is the vacant pedestal, on which he used to stand guard.

Nothing remained of the majestic centaur. Now, on that pedestal, Nothing remains.

No thing.

So these nights, I look up at the sky and see Nothing. While my centaur came and went, I know Nothing will never leave me, for Nothing was... is... and will always be there. Everything comes and goes in the space of Nothing. Forms appear, forms disappear. No thing lasts forever, but Nothing is eternal. Nothing really matters. I don't mean that nothing really matters but, rather, what really matters is Nothing. We are all forms wrapped in the embrace of Nothing. Not only that, a large part of us is Nothing. As a child, I remember playing this little game with myself. I would close my eyes and then ask myself, *What do I see outside? Nothing! What do I see inside of me? Same... Nothing. Can I distinguish between the Nothing outside and the Nothing inside? No, I can't. I can't for the life of me figure out where the Nothing that is inside my skin ends, and where the Nothing that is outside my skin begins. Unless, of course, I touch my skin with my hand.* I recently read that if an atom were taken from a human hand and magnified so much that the nucleus was the size of an apple, the next atom would be 1000 or 2000 miles away. Our bodies would thus be starry skies with the atom being represented by a star, with so much space between the atoms.

We can see how compassionate Nothing is. We take its existence for granted and don't even acknowledge it, but it is always there for us. It is the space that enables the form of words on this page to *be*. Yet, we only read the words; we don't read the space between the words.

Could the centaur… could I too… exist apart from Nothing? Impossible. We had to appear in Nothing. Something can only appear in Nothing, something cannot appear in something. All things come and go but the ever-present Nothing remains. Just as my hero, the centaur, disappeared into Nothing, one realises that the form of this body will also disappear into Nothing one day.

I can rest in the knowing that the formless Nothing is always there. I am inseparable from Nothing. Nothing is my content, which enables me to *be*. At the same time, it remains unaffected by me and all my acrobatics while I exist as an object in time and space. I get close to Nothing in deep sleep, when there is no 'me and my story'. The minute dreaming begins or I wake up, 'me and my story' starts galloping outwards like the centaur, running wild all over the place. The peace of deep sleep is history. How often have I heard people remark when they see the dead body of someone they loved, "Oh, he looks so peaceful!"

He would, for 'he and his story' are dead. All his hopes, fears, stresses, unfulfilled desires, unexpressed thoughts, attachments, regrets of the past, and expectations of the future, all his highs and lows, vanish into Nothing. What remains is peace, just like the peace of deep sleep.

On the subject of attachment, isn't it heartbreaking to keep getting attached to objects that appear in our space, only to have them leave? It could be someone you love, or a possession you cherish, or an image you have of yourself or someone else, that, sooner or later, changes. Have you noticed the Nothing that remains after a particular issue that was occupying your mind and thoughts has been resolved? Or, have you noticed the vacuum of Nothing that remains after you 'lose' something? You lose an object of your affection (a person or thing) and you sense a vacuum deep within, caused by the loss of that object. This is because objects strengthen the identity of the 'me'. We derive our identity from the objects we cherish. No objects to identify with and the strength of the identity weakens. Identification with name and form as a separate entity weakens. Subsequently, the peace of Nothingness shines through. At first, it might be a disconcerting feeling as the 'me' feels it is lacking in something – there is this vast emptiness with which it is unfamiliar. Thereafter, it gets used to this new way of feeling or seeing, or rather, *being* – not being this or that, but simply *being*.

Could one actually *be* the space of Nothing in which everything comes and goes? One needn't even try, for one is already That – the stillness of the Conscious Presence, the eternal witness to 'everything that goes on'. You are already That, or rather, That is already you. Even when you are whirling like a top in your daily living, you are, at the same time, the calm that is the eye of the storm that is the rough and tumble of your daily living. The calm of deep sleep also prevails in the waking state – the only difference being that the 'me and my story' has come in and pitched its tent atop this peace.

All that needs to happen is that the 'me' has to vacate its position for peace to shine through because it is always present and not something to be 'achieved'. The eye of the storm is not separate from the storm. You are that eye, around which is cloaked your personal storm. You have mistakenly identified with the storm alone, taking that to be who you are. But it doesn't matter, for the storm cannot exist separate from its eye. Nothing needs to be done to Nothing. Could Nothing be any more compassionate than that?

I attended the *Kumbh Mela** in March 2010. We had chosen an auspicious bathing date so we would get an opportunity to see the *naga babas***, in all their fervour and frenzy rush to the sacred Ganges river at the appointed hour. On auspicious bathing dates the *Shahi Snaan* or Royal Bath takes place. The leaders and gurus of various sects form a parade, the purpose of which is to take a dip in the Ganges. Crowds throng this parade to seek their blessings. Bands play music and there is euphoria all around. We watched as procession after procession of gurus

---

* Auspicious Hindu festival that is celebrated every six years, with the main Kumbh Mela held every twelve years. It is one of the largest spiritual gatherings of humanity.

** Sect of Shaivite sadhus who remain naked to symbolise their non-attachment to the material world. They rub their bodies with ashes from the holy fires as the symbol of death and rebirth.

seated atop huge, custom-made chariots, and accompanied by ash-smeared sadhus on foot and on horseback, filed past. Whenever they glanced at the crowd, the people would hysterically shout, *"Jai Gurudev! Har Har Mahadev!"** It was an out-of-this-world sight. But what caught me totally by surprise was the next palanquin that came into view. On it was an empty throne and just one disciple standing guard with a royal umbrella. I don't know if the guru had missed getting on due to the huge crowds that were milling around, or whether he had gone to relieve himself, considering that the procession was moving at a snail's pace. It was an ironic sight – but a stark reminder that whether the form is present or absent, Nothing is present on the throne.

Coming back to the centaur, his nature is to go outward – just like that of any human being. The senses project one outward – through sight, taste, smell, hearing and touch. But Chiron, the wise centaur, knows this. He knows that although he is a centaur, and it is in the nature of centaurs to roam wild, at the same time, he is the calm that is the eye of the storm. He has mastered the wild instinct of the centaur on one hand, and the rationality of his human mind on the other. He thus has the capacity to be still. Rooted in the stillness of Nothing, he surveys the world, fixed in one spot. And lest he forget, he takes aim at Nothing too. He is ever vigilant, his bow drawn tight, for Nothing is always all around him. And it is in this stance that he is frozen for Eternity. Not an eternity that means time going on and on endlessly but, rather, the Eternity of the moment – here and now.

---

* Hail to the divine guru! Victory to the Supreme God Shiva!

The wise centaur was consulted by the gods of Olympus and tutored famous demi-gods and Greek heroes. One of them was Achilles, who said, "Brought up in godly Chiron's halls myself, I learned to keep a single heart."

What did Achilles mean by a 'single heart'? Was he referring to 'Consciousness'?

Consciousness is the One Heart. Achilles probably realised that Consciousness is all there is. And that Consciousness is the content of everything. He understood that he, like every other thing, is an object in the same Formless Consciousness. We think we are objects separated from one another. Indeed we are, as objects. But are we truly objects when most of our form is made up of nothing but the presence of Nothing? Isn't it amazing that we human beings have so much of Nothing in common?

Both Nothing and 'something that appears in Nothing' are aspects of Consciousness, but going deeper still, the wise centaur is, in reality, That which enables Nothing as well as something to *be*.

He rests in the knowing that no thing lasts forever, but Nothing lasts forever.

Note:

When Air India was founded in 1948, the management wanted a symbol that denoted speed to a universal audience. The centaur (symbol of Sagittarius in the zodiac), was selected as Air India's logo. A gigantic version of this logo was installed on top of the Air India building in South Mumbai. It used to be lit up in neon blue at night, and the centaur would rotate on its mount very slowly. When Air India underwent a brand makeover, the centaur as the logo was abandoned. Along with that, the neon sign atop Air India's headquarters was brought down.

Watching the centaur from my bedroom window was one of the most cherished memories of my childhood.

THE ETERNAL ECHO

Metamorphosis of Narcissus, Salvador Dali (1937)

An Advaitic (non-dualistic)
interpretation of this painting
is discussed here in the essay
The Eternal Echo.

From the book *Explosion of Love* by Gautam Sachdeva, published in 2011
by Yogi Impressions Books Pvt. Ltd., Mumbai.

THE ETERNAL ECHO

I have been an admirer of surrealist artist Salvador Dali's work since my teenage years. I felt an instant connection with his paintings and would constantly gaze at them in the many coffee table books of his I had purchased or was gifted over the years. I was transfixed by his visual imagery – melting watches, burning giraffes, figures with chests of drawers coming out of them. Dali was an eccentric genius, although some considered him to be nothing more than a brilliant draughtsman. I saw him as an eccentric genius who also happened to be a brilliant draughtsman. Dali had single-handedly changed Sigmund Freud's attitude to surrealism. "This young Spaniard, with his ingenious fanatical eyes and his undoubtedly technically perfect mastership, has suggested to me a different estimate," Freud had once remarked.

One of Dali's most striking paintings is *Metamorphosis of Narcissus.*

There have been several versions of the legend of Narcissus, narrated and interpreted by writers, poets, philosophers and artists. In Greek mythology, Narcissus is a handsome young man renowned throughout the land for his striking good looks. But he consistently disdains those who love him, and treats them with contempt. As Divine punishment, he is made to fall in love with his reflection in a pool, little realising it is his own. He languishes, pines and finally perishes by the pool, not being able to leave the beauty of his own image reflected in the still waters.

Dali's *Metamorphosis of Narcissus*, although measuring just 51 cm × 78 cm, is a staggering work of art. On this canvas, Dali has conveyed the Roman poet Ovid's version of the myth with stunning imagination, brilliance of concept, and skillful execution.

I remember that, while leafing through the books, I would always stop at the page that displayed this painting, struck by the imagery and sheer genius of the man who conceived it. It was perhaps twenty years after my eyes first set sight on it that I understood that Dali, through his version of the metamorphosis of Narcissus, had captured and conveyed the heart of the non-dualistic teaching of the Indian philosophy of Advaita. Whether he realised it or not was irrelevant.

For a better understanding of the deep significance of the painting, we will need to shine the light of Advaita on it. In order to do so, we will also need to take a closer look at Dali – the man and genius – on one hand, and the legend of Narcissus on the other.

The 'Paranoid-Critical' method

Dali has done this painting in his 'Paranoid-Critical' method. No other method could be more apt to portray the myth.

The Paranoid-Critical method was the brainchild of French psychiatrist, Jacques Lacan. He had once spoken to

Dali about his concept, which was meant to put an end to what people thought was real. This in itself is pure Advaita. The world we see is an illusion, an appearance in Consciousness. It is as real or unreal as our dream world.

Dali was taken up with Lacan's concept and developed it further. He even presented his views to a specialist audience at the Sorbonne Center for Aesthetic Studies. Dali explained that, "according to his understanding, paranoia was a complicated delusion in relationships in which the ill person systematically reinterprets the world and the self, ascribing an excessive significance to the self. In contrast to other illnesses, the paranoid person has an orderly, clear, and coherent delusional system. This gives him a feeling of being almighty, which often leads to megalomania or a persecution complex. The aforesaid system operates with hallucinations that reinterpret the phenomena of reality for the benefit of the paranoid person. As a rule, paranoids are physically healthy but mentally live and act in a world of their own, removed from normalcy."*

To illustrate this concept, Dali did a series of paintings in which he showed hidden images within an image. Some examples are *Swans Reflecting Elephants* – in which the reflection of swans on a lake turn out to be elephant figures, and *Phantom Chariot*, which looks like a man is driving a chariot but on closer look, it turns out to be an empty chariot with a town in the distant background, and the figure on the chariot is nothing but a bell-tower in the town.

---

* A detailed account of this extract can be found in the book *Salvador Dali* by Norbert Wolf, Parragon.

Dali could have found no better subject on paranoia than the myth of Narcissus, to display his dexterity in expressing this concept. It was a perfect fit.

The core of the painting

In expressing this myth, Dali shows a young Narcissus kneeling down and staring into the pool, to the left of the painting. The same physical form is placed precisely to the right. However, this time, the body has morphed into a gentle hand of stone, and Narcissus' head has morphed into an egg, held between the finger and thumb of the hand, from which has burst forth a Narcissus flower. Dali could just as well have put his paintbrush down at this stage and the painting would still have been complete, for the concept of spiritual awakening is clearly conveyed in this imagery. The image of identified consciousness (Narcissus the boy) has morphed into an image of impersonal consciousness (Narcissus the flower). Narcissus is reborn as Narcissus. However, 'reborn' is not the accurate word for that implies one thing presaging another. What has actually happened is that his true nature has been revealed with the death of the false sense of identification.

It's all in the name

'Narcissus' – the name is itself one the most important pointers in the entire myth. It means 'sleep' or 'numbness' in Greek.

Sleep – the opposite of Awake, or Spiritually Awake. The myth of Narcissus takes on an important role in psychoanalysis. The term 'Narcissism' denotes an excessive degree of self-esteem or self-involvement. Thus, the ego is numb and asleep, in the sense that it is totally identified with the body and in love with itself as the body. The ego is 'extremely identified' with the name and form of Narcissus as a separate entity – separate from the others. The wave thinks it is separate from the ocean. It does not realise that it is just a short-lived phenomenon on the surface of the ocean, and will sooner or later, merge back into the ocean. It views all other waves as separate from itself, not realising that the content of each wave is the same. Water is the content of the waves, and water is the content of the ocean.

It would seem that Narcissus, with such a name, was doomed to his fate. *Would he ever be able to awaken to his true nature? What would it take to bring him out of this stupor? What would it take for him to realise that the same Consciousness that animates him is what animates others? What would it take for him to learn not to treat others with contempt?*

Could destiny have dealt Narcissus a more unfriendly hand? First, to be named Narcissus and then to be made to fall in love with himself! Or is it too early to judge the myth?

The oracle offers a clue

Lirope – the mother of young Narcissus – was concerned about her handsome son's welfare as he would be the object of everyone's desire. Worried about this, she had consulted the oracle of the land regarding her son's future. The oracle told her that Narcissus would live to a ripe old age, "if he didn't come to know himself."

Here is the second pointer: "If he didn't come to know himself." What could the oracle mean? That Narcissus would die young if he came to know himself? Can anyone die if they come to know themselves? Surely the oracle was not unwise. What could the oracle have meant? What it clearly meant was that if Narcissus would come to know himself, who he was in his true essence, then that would be the end of Narcissus. In other words, Narcissus – as he was someone who treated those who loved him with contempt, could no longer remain the same Narcissus if he truly came to know his true Self.

Echo's heartbreak

In Ovid's version, a nymph called Echo falls in love with Narcissus. One day when Narcissus is out hunting in the forest, Echo stealthily follows him through the woods. She longs to speak with the handsome lad but, of course, is unable to speak first. After a while, Narcissus, upon hearing footsteps behind him, realises that he is being followed. "Who's there?" he exclaims in a loud voice. "Who's there?" answers Echo. This goes on until Echo cannot contain herself any longer and reveals herself to Narcissus, running forward to embrace the handsome youth. But, Narcissus swiftly backs away and asks Echo to leave him alone. He is not interested in reciprocating her love. Narcissus leaves Echo heartbroken and she spends the rest of her lonely life pining away for the love she cannot have – until all that is left is her voice.

"Who's there?" This is the primordial question in Advaita: "Who am I?" as asked by the revered sage Ramana Maharshi. And, "Who is this 'me' who thinks he is the 'doer' of his actions?" as asked by Ramesh Balsekar. "Who's there?" asks Narcissus, only to hear the same words echoed back at him. "Who's there within?" is what Echo is asking

Narcissus, as a response to his own question directed at her. 'Look within – the answer is within; ask your own self "Who's there?"' is what Echo is, in effect, telling Narcissus. But he still doesn't pay heed to the voice he hears. So lost is he in his own self that nothing else seems to penetrate his mind.

Narcissus meets his Nemesis

Enter Nemesis, the goddess who shows no remorse when she expends justice. Incidentally, 'Nemesis' means 'to give what is due' in Greek: Divine retribution. In today's parlance, Nemesis is used to describe one's worst enemy, normally someone or something that is the exact opposite of oneself, but is also somehow similar.

Nemesis, hearing Echo's prayers, decides to punish Narcissus for his obstinate vanity. For Narcissus was a repeat offender who despised and treated with contempt those who fell in love with him.

Walking through the forest one day, he comes across a clear, deep pool. He is thirsty and kneels down to drink its cool water. As he does, he sees his reflection for the first time in his life and instantly falls in love with the beautiful image looking back at him – not realising it is himself!

At that very instant, his fate is sealed. Narcissus is doomed to fall hopelessly in love with his own reflection in the pool. He yearns to possess his mirror image and cannot pull himself away from the beauty of the youth he sees gazing back at him from the depths of the pool. Becoming increasingly sad and forlorn, Narcissus pines by the poolside, the life force in him slowly withering away and eventually, causing his death.

A youth who disdained and shunned the love showered on him by others, has now become the victim of unrequited love.

He had met his Nemesis, or rather, Nemesis had met him.

The end is the beginning

Narcissus died. The oracle had warned that Narcissus would live till a ripe old age, "unless he came to know himself." Obviously, he did not live to a ripe old age, which implies that he came to know himself. What could this possibly mean? Narcissus died, but he came to know himself. Narcissus – totally in love with himself, the most extreme form of identification of the ego with the body – died. It marks the death of identification with a name and form as a separate entity. And, it is nothing but the waters of Consciousness that he sees his image in. Consciousness is his mirror, and he gazes long and hard into it. And then, what is reflected back at him is the reality of who he truly is.

Narcissus is reborn as Narcissus

In the spot where he died, the Narcissus flower grew. A Narcissus flower – with no sense of separation. A flower that is not aware that it is an object of beauty. A flower that gives its fragrance equally to all who come near it. A flower that does not treat others with contempt, for in its world there are no others. No others to love, no others to hate. Impersonal consciousness. The identified consciousness that was earlier represented by Narcissus – the handsome boy – on one hand, is now re-presented as the impersonal consciousness of Narcissus – the flower – on the other. The wave in essence is not separate from the ocean, and the content of the wave and that of the ocean is the same – water. And that water is Consciousness.

What's more, in Dali's depiction, the flower bursts forth from an egg, clearly signifying the rebirth of Narcissus. And the egg is juxtaposed in direct visual correspondence to the boy's head – symbolising the ego. Could it be any more obvious? Could Dali have made it any clearer without using words?

Dali wrote a poem on this theme in which he stated that in Catalonia, the phrase 'to have a bulb in the head' meant to have a psychological complex. With fluid grace, Narcissus's head turns into an egg, a bulb. And the bulb turns into a flower. No other visual sequence could be more perfect.

And what could be considered a glorious coup is the fact that when Narcissus kneels down to look at his reflection, he assumes the foetal position. And it is from the waters of Consciousness, which now take on the role of the amniotic fluid, that he is born again in foetal form for the hand is exactly in the same pose as Narcissus. One cycle of death and birth is complete. The Ouroborus returns to remind us that the end is the beginning.

Why is Narcissus, the good looking lad, depicted kneeling down in the foetal position; a position assumed by the baby before it is born? Wasn't Narcissus the one who thought he was exceedingly good looking? Wasn't he the one who scorned anyone who loved him? Then, how could he be shown with such innocence when he created so much misery for others?

The fact was, Narcissus did not choose to be good looking. Nor did he choose to fall in love with himself upon looking at his reflection. He was made to – by the intervention of Nemesis. Narcissus was not the most extreme form of identified consciousness (identification with the body) by choice, and nor was the rebirth of Narcissus as impersonal consciousness by choice. Both events were happenings, which were dependent on factors not in his control. Both were events orchestrated by Consciousness.

Consciousness is depicted as identified consciousness through Narcissus the good-looking boy. Upon deep reflection – an act orchestrated by Consciousness through the intervention of Nemesis – the ego cracked and from the crack bloomed the Narcissus flower – Consciousness as impersonal consciousness. It was all along a play of Consciousness. What else could Narcissus be if not innocent? It is important to note that Narcissus did not *do* anything to be born again. It was a happening orchestrated by Consciousness.

The return of Echo

Echo, a divine spirit, is not forgotten in all of this. She is very much part of the picture. For the hand being structurally a replica of Narcissus's kneeling pose, is nothing but an 'echo' of the same. It is Narcissus' echo that is the hand that holds the egg from which the Narcissus flower bursts forth. Echo becomes the cradle of a hand that gently holds the egg between its thumb and finger. Both the dualities of male and female come together literally. For on one side is Narcissus the boy and on the other, the echo of Narcissus the boy. They are, in effect, not two.

The duality of life

In fact, this duality of life, including the duality of male and female, is what is consistently reflected in the background of the painting. In the background is a hero perched on his pedestal who thinks he is the master of his destiny. His back is facing us and he looks lonely. In turn, the pedestal is placed in the centre of black and white squares, resembling a chessboard.

It is the chessboard of life, the black and white representing the world of duality, choices to be made, failure and victory, pleasures and pains. On his left, the nudes represent the sensual pleasures that abound in life. Pleasure's opposite is also depicted in the form of an unhealthy, malnourished dog feeding on fresh meat – a symbol of both decay and hunger. However, his desire for food seems to have been met for now. Dead meat gives life to the dog, once again depicting the eternal cycle of life. In the distance is a road, signifying life's journey. Thematically, Dali is representing the cycle of daily living that is mired in the duality of opposites, the context in which the metamorphosis of Narcissus takes place.

Depicted far beyond are the hills of enlightenment. Behind them, an image of another stone hand is once again repeated, though this time it is only partially visible, 'echoing' the fact that enlightenment is at hand. But the hero is too busy looking down to even notice it is there; he is too caught up in the game of life.

Salvador Dali, Narcissus and Advaita

So, where does this leave Dali in relation to the painting? Dali takes on the role of the Creator who lays bare this Paranoid-Critical world of his – worlds within worlds, images within images, constructs of the imagination far removed from reality. Dali would thus, by himself creating the delusory world of Narcissus, become the ultimate Narcissus (which he was accused of in any case by his detractors). We even have Narcissus bowing down in front of the artist as Creator, a subtle acknowledgement of the Creator-Subject (the Source) by the created object. It is said that Dali did his best to make use of the thought processes of the mentally ill for his art, by adapting them as far as possible without himself going insane. It is no wonder then that he declared: "The only difference between me and a madman is that I am not mad." It could just as well be a deeply profound statement of Advaita.

It is seen that while the entire myth is played out in a linear sequence of events, from the boy falling in love with himself to transforming into a flower, Dali has achieved the same in one instant. The horizontal time-sequence is seen all at once in the painting, 'in vertical time', in the Now. Naturally, the viewer, being placed outside the context of the painting, is able to view all of its contents at once, including all the characters therein. For the viewer, all events exist simultaneously on the canvas... there is truly no past and future, though there appears to be in the myth. This is an important pointer – that the identified consciousness and the impersonal consciousness are not two. Due credit must be given to Dali for this default virtue of the painting. For it would take nothing less than the mind of a genius to execute this myth through the brilliance of such a concept, painted onto a canvas.

But, at the end of it all, Consciousness is the Ultimate

Creator – the Source of all there is. For Consciousness is Dali, Consciousness is Narcissus the boy, Consciousness is Narcissus the flower, Consciousness is Ovid, Consciousness is the canvas, the paint and the paintbrush, and Consciousness is viewing the painting through the eyes of the viewer. Without Dali being conscious in the first place, the painting would never have happened. The true genius behind Dali's expression of the myth of Narcissus is Consciousness. 'When a flag flutters in the breeze, it is neither the flag nor the breeze that has any causal significance, but the Consciousness in which the event took place,' an old Zen saying points out.

In understanding the deeper meaning of this piece of art within the context of Advaita, the light of Consciousness shines upon the painting, which in turn *echoes* back, bringing alive the incredible gift that is the teaching of A-dvaita – not-two. The myth of Narcissus is a vivid illustration of this philosophy. The myth is far more than 'a cautionary tale warning boys against being cruel to their lovers'. For their 'lover', reflected in the pure waters of Consciousness, is none other than their Self.

Consciousness is all there is.

THE END OF DUALITY

One of the most precious gifts I received while being with my teacher, Ramesh Balsekar, for almost ten years, was to be there with him during the last few months of his life. It was a tremendous learning experience to see someone so comfortable with dying. The ease with which he had lived each day was the same ease he now felt about dying. He used to say, "If one is not afraid of living, then one will not be afraid of dying."

Ramesh passed away at the ripe old age of ninety-two. Ten years ago, when I had started attending his talks, he used to tell visitors, "I am in the transit lounge." Well, he was in the transit lounge for much longer than he anticipated. He would often say that he was ready to go 'home' anytime, and did not care whatever happened in the next moment. He would quote an old Zen *roshi* (elder master), "Forgive me for not dying," and let out a booming laugh!

It was only in the last year or so that his health started declining. However, each time he had a fall or visited the hospital, he was promptly back on his feet. He couldn't wait to start speaking at the daily satsangs and would often not heed the advice of his doctor or his beloved wife Sharda to rest some more until he got his strength back. The satsangs were clearly what kept him going. I remember the time when he had a fall and got a big black eye as a result. Apart from the fact that it looked quite ugly, he did not feel much discomfort. I casually went into his room one morning before satsang to say hello. During these mornings, DVDs were played of his previous talks, while he rested in the room. Knowing that in all probability he wouldn't speak, I still found myself asking, "Guruji, will you speak today?" Before he could answer, Sharda replied in her protective voice, "He needs to rest." I asked him if he felt any discomfort and he said no. Then pointing to the black eye he said, "But look at this!" I said that it wouldn't bother us in the least bit, and if it didn't bother him then he should come out and speak. I knew I had crossed a certain line with his wife, but I also knew he looked forward to speaking. "You're right," he replied. And he was out in the living room in five minutes, for yet another satsang.

However, as the months passed, it took a bit of coaxing to get Ramesh to come into the living room to speak. What's more, he had started saying, "What had to be said has been said." I was informed that usually when a master passes a statement like this, he is giving his disciples a sign that he won't be around much longer. It is traditionally said that after such a sign is provided, masters are known to have dropped their body within six months. Another incident I took as a subtle sign was when, one day, I saw a pile of books lying on a table in Ramesh's verandah. Ramesh was giving away all his books from his personal collection, and anyone was free to take one or more. This I took as a clear sign of things to come.

Some mornings, we used to see his assistant having to literally hold him while he walked into the living room from his bedroom, his feet dragging heavily across the floor. It was a painful sight for us to witness. His body was losing its energy. Nevertheless, Ramesh couldn't have been bothered in the least, as long as he could make it to the rocking chair on which he used to sit and give satsang. In a way, it was a delight to see his enthusiasm; his mind was sharp and he was as clear as always. Once he was in the chair, the teaching simply flowed through him.

During this time, the subject of the talks invariably revolved around death. This happened in a spontaneous, unplanned way. A new seeker would come for the satsang and ask a question related to death, even though he was clueless about Ramesh's precarious condition. Somehow, Consciousness manoeuvred the conversations so that this subject was brought up. Ramesh's answers were short, as he did not have much energy. But one statement he used to constantly utter was: "I don't understand what is the big deal about death. After all, isn't death the end of duality – the end of the pleasures and pains of daily living? Who wouldn't want that?" Someone asked him, "At this stage in life, do you have any unfulfilled desires?" He replied, "None. But a new one has arisen. I want to die. But at the same time, I know it will happen when it is supposed to happen." And then he would laugh.

I was quite amazed as well as amused to witness Ramesh's attitude towards his death. What a refreshing perspective it was! No fears associated with what was inevitable, rather a welcoming of it – just like a weary traveller who looks forward to a good night's sleep. In one of his talks, when someone asked him how he felt about dying, he said, "I don't look forward to it, but I welcome it."

Over these last days I would, like other disciples, visit him at his home and in the hospital. Three such visits to the hospital struck me. While I was away in London, he had been admitted to the ICU. As soon as I returned, I went to see him. He was sitting up in bed. There wasn't much to say but I knew something had changed. He asked me how my trip was and then fell silent. Standing beside his bed, I asked him after some time, "Guruji, are you tired of all this?" He looked at me and said, "Yes," with a gentle, fleeting smile. It was from then on that I started wishing he would go 'home' sooner rather than later, so he wouldn't have to suffer much more.

On another trip to the hospital, I asked him whether he was getting bored of lying in bed all day for so many days. He raised his hands and replied, "Witnessing is happening. But yes, I'd like to go home."

It was the next visit that was the last straw for me. I went to see him in the afternoon, thanks to a visitor's pass given to me by a family member. I was sitting in the room with him and a nurse barged in. It was time for his medication. She was rough. And, she was loud. She spoke to him in Marathi and said words to this effect: "Come on old man, it is time for your medication and let's make it fast. I have other things to do, so don't waste my time." The sharp tone of her voice and the way in which she administered the medicine was heartbreaking. I wondered whether I should say anything to her but then I thought, 'What's the point?' My only consolation was knowing that she too was 'being lived' to be the way she was. God alone knows what stress she must be going through at work during the day. That's when I closed my eyes and said a silent prayer to God, to let the end come soon.

During these last few months, I had started attending Ramesh's talks on Saturdays in addition to the Sundays when I would regularly go. Now that I felt there wasn't much time left, I stopped going to work on Saturdays and instead, attended the talks. I remember, on my second visit to him ten years ago, he told me at the end of the talks, "Be careful... you have come two Sundays in a row... this could become your Sunday church!" – which it eventually did.

Now that he was really unwell even my travel plans out of town depended on his health. I saw to it that I made short trips. Before each trip I would visit him and tell him where I was going and when I would be back. Of course, this was done for my own satisfaction; Ramesh was not really concerned about the details of my itinerary. Nevertheless, it felt good to keep him informed.

One particular weekend in June, I found Ramesh's talks quite powerful. They were short – lasting about twenty minutes instead of the usual ninety minutes, and were punctuated by long gaps of potent silence. After the talk on Sunday, I went into his room and told him what I felt about the talks over the last two days. I said that the thought came to me of getting them transcribed, and when I shared it with Sanjay, a friend and another long-time disciple of Ramesh, he seconded the idea. Ramesh was thrilled to hear this and said, "I was thinking of exactly the same thing."

Two days later, Ramesh lost his dear wife Sharda in the early hours of the morning. She was ninety and they had been married sixty-nine years. That afternoon, I went over to visit him. I entered his room and saw him sitting in his chair by the window, calm and serene. The lightness in the air was ethereal, as was the light of the afternoon sun that gently streamed into the room through the curtain. Somehow, it did not feel like Sharda had passed away. It was as though she was sitting in the chair next to him exactly the way they always sat over the years. Ramesh perked up and said, "I talk on death over the weekend, and see what happens!" A moment later, the phone rang. It was a condolence call. Ramesh listened into the phone and kept saying, "Yes… yes…" Then, his face lit up with a smile and he said to the person at the other end of the line, "Can you imagine? We were told our horoscopes matched. It is no wonder that we were married for sixty-nine years!" He was the picture of equanimity that day. In fact, it half-seemed as though Ramesh was offering condolences to the person at the other end.

When I felt it was time to leave, I got up and not knowing what to say or do, I just knelt in front of him and put my head in his lap. The next thing I knew, he was patting me on the back of my head as if to say, 'It's okay, my child, it's okay…' I thought the situation was comic yet profound. When I raised my head and got up to leave, he suddenly enquired, "Can you find out?" "Sure, what?" I asked. "I wonder how long I have." I had a flummoxed look on my face though I knew quite well what he meant. He then let out a small laugh and said, "Never mind… I was just curious." And I thought, 'As though the situation isn't surreal enough!'

I went home and mentioned this to my mother. I also wondered whether it would be appropriate to ask some astrologers about how much more time Ramesh had left. She said that it would not be appropriate to ask such a question and, what's more, no authentic astrologer would provide an answer for that would mean playing God. Nevertheless, I felt that since Ramesh had asked me, I should make an attempt at least to find out. Access to astrologers was relatively easy since, being on the spiritual path even in terms of the book publishing business, I had the good fortune of meeting many. And so, the next day I asked a few astrologers how much time they thought Ramesh had left. In doing so, I just proved my mother right. The astrologers initially said that it was not appropriate for them to comment on it, especially as according to them, someone like Ramesh could, to a large extent, influence the process of determining when to leave (so much for Ramesh's teaching on 'non-doership'). Anyway, I had done my bit so to speak.

However, the next day I was pleasantly surprised to get feedback from all of them. They were quite unanimous in predicting that October would be a difficult month for Ramesh. In fact, they said that if Ramesh were to see October through, then he would probably live on for another couple of years. I knew I had the answer, for it was clear just how eager Ramesh was to 'merge into the pool of Consciousness' as he often said.

The following Sunday, I went into Ramesh's room and mentioned to him, "Guruji, I found out what you asked me to..." He looked a bit puzzled, as if he had no idea what I was talking about. It had probably slipped his mind. And then I added, "They said that you need to take care of your health in October." So much for my subtlety. Ramesh was quick to pick up the cue, and had his answer. He looked a bit dejected. "October?" he said, "Let's see..." He started counting the months on his fingers... "July, August, September... still three more months?" I was nonplussed. Here he was, actually counting the days till his departure, and not being happy with the fact that it was still three months away. He saw the surprised look on my face and folding his hands in a 'namaste' said, "Thank you, Gautam. You have no idea what a beautiful gift death is." I returned the namaste with a heavy heart, and quietly left the room.

Ramesh used to say that it was Sharda's wish that she should go before Ramesh, for she could not bear to see him die. And that is exactly what happened. Once she passed away, it was clear that Ramesh would not hang around for long and so, the prospect of losing him in October became more and more real.

All this time, I was working hard to get the transcripts ready for what I knew was the last book I was working on with him. The deadline was set by Consciousness, if the astrologers turned out to be accurate: October. Ramesh had asked me to also transcribe his two talks given after Sharda passed away as he felt they formed a set. I jokingly told him, "Only two more..." He laughed. He had this habit of adding more and more notes or transcripts to a manuscript that was supposedly ready for printing. He would say with all sincerity, "Gautam, if we make the book a little thicker, we can charge more!" Always the banker, Ramesh.

I recall visiting him one day after work, for some clarifications on the manuscript. I called his home and asked his daughter Jaya, who was visiting him from Bangalore, if I could come over. I went across but, by the time I reached there, some members of their family had dropped in to pay a visit. I stood in the verandah till their conversation ended. Ramesh spotted me and when he saw the manuscript in my hands, his eyes lit up. Midway through the conversation he got up and started walking towards two empty chairs, gesturing to me. He had no energy to do so on his own and his attendant rushed in, lest he fell. I felt embarrassed as I had broken into the conversation, but I knew Ramesh's priority was the teaching. We swiftly went through the text, and then I left.

Throughout these last few months, I made it a point to express gratitude to Ramesh for his impact on my life. I remember that when my mother's guru passed away, she was fortunate that she happened to see him during his last days without knowing that those were his final days. It gave her a tremendous sense of completion. I knew Ramesh's time was approaching, and so I began thanking him for all things big and small.

I remember once I had said that thanks to him and the satsangs I had made so many friends the world over and, what's more, they were friends who were close and stayed in touch. He looked at me, smiled and said, "It's a happening." On another occasion, I told him that I was wondering where I got the confidence to write. Then the memory arose of the Foreword I had written for the first book I worked on with him – *The Ultimate Understanding*. I was compelled to write the Foreword. I even remember telling my mother, "What if he thinks it's really bad? Would I be putting him in an awkward position?" Nevertheless, I mustered the courage to send it across. The next day, the envelope came back. It looked like he hadn't opened it at all. Even the two A4 size sheets did not look like they had been unfolded. I looked at the first one and saw no note or remark from him. I flipped it over to check the next one and, to my delight, I found a post-it note on which he had written, *Excellent! Thanks. RSB.* I told Ramesh that it was now quite clear to me that it was his note that gave me the confidence to write subsequently, and so I thanked him for the same. Once again he smiled and said, "It's a happening."

That's what I loved about Ramesh. He was a fount of impersonal love. There was no stickiness. There was no give and take. There was no 'you' and 'me'. Everything was a happening that was supposed to happen because it was God's will. If it was not meant to happen, no power on earth could make it happen. If it was meant to happen, no power on earth could prevent it from happening. We are just instruments through whom Consciousness functions. Who is to thank whom and for what? Once, when I had gone across to my mom's guru's meditation session, someone had, at the end of it, thanked him for the wonderful meditation. To this he replied, "Thanking me is like your left hand thanking your right hand."

On one of my visits, I thought I would tell Ramesh that I would do my best to see that his books stayed in print. Now both he and I knew that that was stating the obvious. I generally don't believe that everything needs to be stated, and I know that the obvious certainly need not be stated to be heard. Perhaps, it is heard louder when it isn't stated – words can, at times, water down the sanctity of the silence of a deeply profound knowing.

Still, the need arose to state it to the 'Divine banker', for the record as it were. He let out a most feeble 'thank you' and smiled. It was more like, 'Of course I knew that you would, but in any case as you are being formal, so will I'. I then told him, "Thanking me is like your left hand thanking your right hand." I was dying to use this phrase, and got the opportunity. We both had a hearty laugh.

The end of September arrived. One Friday, I visited Ramesh. I had actually planned to visit him the following day, Saturday, but his daughter Jaya called and said she was returning to Bangalore on Saturday, and wanted to hand me her father's notes written over the years. Although I could have collected these notes when I went there on Saturday, I thought it would be a good opportunity to visit them on Friday and meet Jaya as well.

I left work early, and reached Ramesh's home in good time. I first went into the room to sit with Ramesh. He had been drifting for a while in and out of what I could best describe as an 'altered state'. I was carrying the new cover design of his book *The End of Duality*. The book was almost ready. I knew he was really in no condition to see it or comment on it. Nevertheless I just wanted to let him know – at any level – that the book was 'happening'. I had been keeping him updated on its progress over the last few weeks, but I also knew how happy he was every time he saw the cover of one of his new books. He loved commenting on the creative aspect of the books on which we worked together. His attendant informed me that the right time to speak to Ramesh was when he would turn in his bed, as the effort of doing so made him a bit more alert. So, I sat beside him and when he was about to turn, in a voice louder than usual, I said, "Guruji, this is the cover of your new book." I held it in front of his eyes so that he didn't have to strain. His eyes opened, lit up, and he smiled, and in all of twenty seconds he slipped back into his semi-conscious state. I thought to myself that he really couldn't be bothered about the book at this stage, yet he had managed a smile. It was incredible!

In one hand I was holding the book, and with the other I was holding his hand. He was restless and kept turning sides constantly. I waited for the opportune moment to release my hand. I remember thinking how strong his grip was in spite of his weak condition. Not surprising though, considering he had been a body-builder in his younger days.

On Sunday morning, while getting ready for satsang, I was just lighting some incense in my bedroom when the phone rang. It was Jaya. She said she had just spoken with Shivdas, her brother, who told her that Ramesh's condition had deteriorated. She said I should be prepared. I told her I would leave immediately and go across, but she said that perhaps I would not want to see him suffering. I said that I just had to go. I got ready and was at the door when my phone rang again. I rushed back and it was Chaitanya – Ramesh's younger brother. In a tearful voice he said, "My brother just passed away."

I used to drive to Ramesh's home, but that day, afraid that I might not find parking space easily, I jumped into a taxi. It usually isn't easy to find one in my lane on an early Sunday morning, so I thanked my stars when one approached me. It seemed like the longest drive to Sindhula (the name of Ramesh's building), although it took the usual time. The building's watchman had no clue as to what had happened upstairs, and told me as I entered: *"Saab, aaj aap jaldi aa gaye"* (You have come early today). Upon entering the apartment, I saw Shivdas and some members of the family in the living room. I went into the bedroom, kissed Ramesh on the forehead, and sat next to him for a while. Suddenly, the memory came up of something he had said to me many years ago: "Don't run after the taxi. Let the taxi come to you!" I don't know whether it is possible to laugh and cry at the same time, but I think that's what happened to me.

Family, friends and disciples streamed into Sindhula throughout the day, to say their goodbyes. We also sang bhajans in his bedroom.

We left for the funeral grounds at around 5 p.m. and the funeral took place around 9 p.m. There were no rituals performed as Ramesh did not believe in them. We placed a few garlands on him and gave him a quiet send-off.

It was only the next day that the memory arose of what one of the astrologers had mentioned to me. A few days after he had said that the month of October would be difficult, he had called me up and said that after studying the charts further, it seemed there was a window of a possibility of Ramesh leaving between the 21st and 27th of September. He said that those days offered a soft nudge into the other world as far as Ramesh's chart was concerned. While it would not have any impact on most of us who need a 'push' or a 'shove' to cross over, a gentle nudge was perhaps all that was needed for someone like Ramesh, and in any case, he was eager to leave. Of course, I never mentioned this to Ramesh for I felt there was hardly any difference between the end of September and October. Ramesh passed away on the 27th of September.

After his passing, I started picking up his earlier books to read – the ones he had written much before I met him. Barring a few, I had not read most of them and was now thoroughly enjoying reading them. In a way, I was glad that I hadn't read them earlier for I was able to appreciate them all the more now, after having spent ten years in personal contact with him. One night, before switching off the lights, I was lying in bed reading his book *A Duet of One – The Ashtavakra Gita Dialogue* (1989). I sat bolt upright when I read the following passage:

"In 'Thus Spake Zarathustra' by Friedrich Nietzsche, Zarathustra gives his disciples the ultimate message: Whatever had to be said has been said; whatever had to be understood has been understood. Now forget whatever has been said. Forget everything I have said except this last message. Beware of Zarathustra!"

In quoting this paragraph, Ramesh was pointing to the fact that a teaching should not be just an intellectual understanding, but something tested in the fire of one's personal experience. He was driving home the fact that there is always a limit to what can be gathered intellectually by listening to a master's words. This is what Zarathustra meant when he said, 'Beware of Zarathustra'. Rather, one must *live* the teaching. What it is pointing to is: Be Aware of Zarathustra.

While this essay was taking shape, my friend Gabriel

sent me a snippet of something Ramesh had said during one of the talks, that appealed to him. It was on the subject of death, and Gabriel's mail came at the most appropriate time. It said:

"You have to be there to contemplate the terror of death and your impending absence therewith! Paradoxical, that you must be present first to give rise to the terror of your absence! In fact, the thought of not being here can only be contemplated precisely because you are always here! So death is an idea of absence within your presence!"

During one of the last satsangs of Ramesh, he used the term *'Vishal Hriday'*.

What is Vishal Hriday? It literally translates as 'Big Heart'. What it actually means is 'One Heart'. To place it in the context of his teaching, it translates as 'All there is, is Consciousness'.

Consciousness functions through each one of us; we are instruments through whom the same Consciousness functions. Nobody truly 'does' anything, but all events are a happening that had to happen according to the will of God… the Source… Consciousness. There is no 'other' to blame, condemn, or hate. When there is no 'other' to hate, there is truly no 'other'. When there is no 'other' there is no 'me' as well, separate from the 'other'. When there is no 'me' or 'other', then *everything* is all there is – and all is exactly as it is supposed to be in that moment. This is impersonal love: the absence of separation. Impersonal, for there is no 'other' separate from 'me' to love personally. *Living* this understanding (not just thinking it) is Vishal Hriday – a total acceptance of 'what is': acceptance of people exactly the way they are – including oneself, of situations exactly the way they are, and even of death – the end of the existence of 'me' as a separate entity.

Could there be a greater love than accepting whatever life brings in the next moment? Could there be a greater love than accepting people exactly the way they are? Could there be a greater love than not hating anyone? Ramesh used to say, "I'm not telling you to love everyone. All I am saying is, just don't hate anyone."

No more Ramesh.

No more Sunday church.

It is *the end of duality* for him.

The river has merged with the ocean.

What was a reality for ten years is now consigned to the vaults of my memory. And whenever a memory of Ramesh does arise, it brings forth a smile and a tear at the same time. 'Where do they come from?' I wonder. Where else, but from where Ramesh has always been, and always will be: the Heart. Not the one pumping in the left side of the chest, but the Heart of hearts – Vishal Hriday. Consciousness.

CONSCIOUSNESS AND THE FENIX

The phoenix is a mythical bird believed to have a lifespan of five hundred years. When it nears the end of its long life, it builds a nest, sits in it, and then self-ignites; enacting what seems like a spontaneous combustion. Both the phoenix and its nest go up in a blaze of glory and are reduced to ashes. From these ashes, a young phoenix is born, to live again for another complete lifespan. The young phoenix embalms the ashes of its old self in an egg and flies with it to the Egyptian city of Heliopolis – the Sun City – where it places it in the temple of the Sun.

The phoenix is considered an emanation of sunlight. It is a symbol of immortality through resurrection.

The end is the beginning.

It was a regular Wednesday. I came home from work, around 7 p.m. My mother walked in a bit later, and put a bag full of incense sticks on the table in my bedroom. She said it was a birthday gift for me from Alan whom she had met at the meditation she just attended.

After a while, I called up The Oberoi Hotel where he was staying to thank him. Strangely, the phone lines just kept ringing and I was unable to get through.

Little did I know that Alan had been shot and lay dead on the floor of the hotel.

Consciousness chooses the venue

This was the second visit that Master Charles Cannon made to India in 2008, to introduce his meditation technology. Master Charles had lived in India for over twelve years in his younger days. He had spent time with Swami Muktananda, a Siddha Yoga master who was in turn the disciple of the renowned Indian sage Bhagavan Nityananda of Ganeshpuri.

The first time Master Charles visited India to introduce his technology was in February of the same year. My publishing team had helped organise the event. It was a success – over two hundred people had attended the programme. This provided ample encouragement to Master Charles and the Synchronicity group, and before we knew it, the next event was scheduled for November 2008. We did mention that it might be a good idea to postpone the event, perhaps to the following year, considering the first one took place at the beginning of the same year. But plans for the second event had gathered a momentum of their own, and November was the month decided upon by Master Charles as he had another engagement to attend in Mumbai at the same time.

This time, he was coming with a group of over twenty meditators who followed the Synchronicity programme. They were converging on Mumbai from different parts of the world. We were asked to help select a hotel for the group. We decided on The President Hotel for their stay while they were in Mumbai, as the hotel offered a good group rate and was close to the venue where the programmes were to be held. However, at virtually the last minute, a representative of The Oberoi Hotel, whom we were also in talks with earlier as it was the preferred choice, called us up and matched the rate, as they were keen to host Master Charles and his group at their hotel. It was a non-issue; The Oberoi was also close to the venue and it offered a splendid view of the Arabian Sea.

Compassionate Consciousness fulfils the wish

Alan, Vice President of Synchronicity, had made a trip to Mumbai on his own, earlier in June to plan the forthcoming event in November. As he was here for over a week, we were able to spend some quality time with him. Being a meditator for over twenty-five years, and having been with Maharishi Mahesh Yogi before meeting Master Charles, he was firmly rooted in spiritual life. Added to this was the fact that he was a practising Vedic astrologer. A font of spiritual wisdom and a marvellous storyteller, Alan would regale us with anecdotes over the meals that we shared.

Alan loved India with all his heart. He enjoyed walking the streets of Mumbai, taking in the sights and sounds, and treating himself to an occasional *paan* (betel-leaf) by the roadside, or a *kulfi* (Indian ice cream).

One day he casually said, "Oh, I would love to die in India."

His wish was fulfilled in just a few months. It reminds me of the saying: 'Be careful what you ask for; you might just get it'. The only trouble is we can't choose *how* we will get it.

It was Alan's thirteen-year-old daughter Naomi's first

visit to India. She had accompanied him and was having a wonderful time with most of the Synchronicity meditators doting on her, buying her gifts and calling her their little 'angel'. She always wanted her nose pierced, and she now had her wish fulfilled in India. My mother gifted her silver *payals* – a set of anklets. She had been wondering whether to give them to Naomi as a parting gift at the end of her trip. For some reason, she had decided not to wait but give them now. Naomi, with her pierced nose, payals and Indian kurtas, thoroughly enjoyed her new avatar.

At the meditation session, before heading back to the hotel, Naomi asked my mother, "Am I spiritual?" To us it seemed that for a thirteen-year-old, born to parents who were living in a spiritual community, it should have perhaps been obvious. But, it was the innocence of a child's mind that made her ask the question. It reminds me of what my teacher Ramesh would often say: "True humility is not recognised as such by the one who has it."

This question might have been in the child's mind for a while. Perhaps she wanted an answer from 'outside' her environment, which is why she asked my mother. My mother replied, "Yes, and you're having a human experience."

Naomi had her answer. And, she also had the wish of getting her nose pierced fulfilled.

The event has already happened

Naomi, the little angel, was quite a special child. She was blessed with a gifted vision – for she could see angelic beings, as well as have visions of masters in other realms. She would describe her vision and when she would be shown a likely picture of the saint or spiritual master, she would be able to identify the personage. For example, she described one such vision and then when she was shown an image of St. Francis of Assisi, she confirmed it was him. At first, she thought everyone could see these ethereal beings. It was only later she realised that just a few could see what she saw.

While she was in India, she was well looked after by the Synchronicity group, but what was truly wonderful to see was the love showered on her by her father. Rarely had I seen such an expressive display of love and affection between father and daughter.

Two weeks before her trip to India, Naomi woke up from a nightmare she had. She went and told her mother that she had a dream in which she was having a meal at a restaurant with her father when gunmen came and shot them down.

Could there have been more obvious evidence to support the fact that the event had already taken place in the future?

The return of the Master

In the days between the introductory talk and the main event that was planned for Master Charles, small satsangs used to take place every evening. The Synchronicity group would be present, along with people from Mumbai who were interested in attending them. The evenings included small meditations, listening to meditation music and some chanting.

On the evening of the terrorist attacks, a few of the students from my mother's meditation group also attended the satsang. One of them is gifted in her own special way, and has had some experiences that could be termed 'paranormal'. After the session, she reached home and called my mother to inform her of something strange she witnessed. She mentioned that during the meditation, she saw the form of Master Charles' guru Swami Muktananda (1908-1982) standing behind him. She asked him, telepathically, "What are you doing here?" He answered, in Marathi, "I have come because of him" (pointing to Master Charles). She had no clue what this exchange meant.

The answer was provided within the hour.

Consciousness takes the decisions

On this particular day, after the evening meditation, Master Charles was dropped back at the hotel and went up to his room. The rest of the group decided to walk back. They usually took taxis back but that evening a walk seemed in order. While they normally had dinner at the hotel, some of them thought of dining at a nearby restaurant. However, this plan got scuttled and they headed to the Tiffin restaurant in The Oberoi. Because they were at the restaurant later than their usual time, they were there when the terrorists arrived. Had it not been for this change in plan, they would have already finished the meal and been up in their rooms, like the other members of the group.

Who decided that they walk back? Who decided they would get late because they walked back? Who decided that they eat at the Tiffin restaurant and no other restaurant? Who decided that they stay at The Oberoi in the first place? Who decided the dates on which they would be in Mumbai? Were they decisions taken by individuals, or was it a force that had weaved together a series of events in order for them to be in Mumbai, on this date of the year, in this hotel, at this exact time, in this particular restaurant?

They were disappointed that their regular table at the front of the restaurant was taken because they had reached late. They had to settle for a table at the back. If they had been at their usual table, in all probability none would have survived.

The smoke of illusion

When I reached home from work that evening, I was pleasantly surprised to find a bag full of incense sticks lying in my room. I had celebrated my birthday just two days before and this was a birthday gift from Alan. I decided to call the hotel and thank him. Strangely, the numbers just kept ringing. The television in my room was on, with the sound muted. I kept trying but no one was picking up the phone. Then I saw a newsflash on TV that said some gang wars had broken out, and there was firing outside The Oberoi as well as The Taj. I did not connect this piece of information with the fact that the phone simply kept ringing. It was a bit later that the news anchor announced that it was a terrorist attack.

We were up for most of the night watching the TV for any news that we could get. What a surreal night it was. Reality TV, so to speak. Everything was in real time, live on television. In the medieval ages, it would perhaps take a month for this kind of news to reach people. If a castle was attacked in France, it would be weeks before the news would reach England. Now, thanks to technology, everything was happening 'live' in our bedrooms. That is why everything seems amplified – we feel we are part of the happening even though we are witnessing it from a distance. When people remark, "Oh, look what the world is coming to… all these wars, terrorism…" – one sometimes wonders: Is the world any worse than what it has been down the ages? What about the Crusades? The World Wars? People being burnt at stakes, flayed alive, their limbs tied to four horses that then run in different directions, or cities being bombed out… how much worse are things, really? The only difference is that events are now being witnessed by us as they are happening in real time. Imagine how ghastly it would be to see people being burnt alive at the stake, on your television, while you are lying in your bed having potato chips!

The Oberoi Hotel is a five-minute walk from my home. I could hear the 'Boom!' of the grenades that were being thrown into the lobby of the hotel, while at the same time watching the news anchor reporting from the scene and saying that grenades were exploding. I heard the live boom seconds before the same boom was heard on the TV. 'Is this for real or what?' I wondered.

We were finally able to make contact with Master Charles on his mobile phone and kept updating him with the latest news we saw on TV, throughout the night. Neither the TVs in the hotel nor their telephone lines were functioning. They had been disconnected. Therefore, they had no clue about what was going on. The rest of the Synchronicity group were holed up in their rooms and had barricaded their doors. One lone member also heard a key being inserted into the keyhole of her room door. 'Click-click! Click-click!' It moved to the left and the right, and then the person moved on. You can imagine what must have gone through her mind – 'was the hand manipulating the key friendly or hostile?' She decided to take no chances and did not respond. If she had, then perhaps she would not have lived to tell the tale.

They never knew what the next moment would bring – a barrage of gunfire, bombs going off, someone knocking on their door, smoke seeping in through the gap below the door… what would happen next? There is a saying, 'If you think things can't get worse, it's probably only because you lack sufficient imagination'. Smoke started filling the rooms and it got difficult to breathe. Some members of the Synchronicity group used the brass lamp in their room to break the window glass; others, the ironing board. The air conditioning went off, the electricity went out, the water supply dwindled… no matter how much 'positive thinking' you were into, you wouldn't blame them for imagining things could get worse.

While watching TV, we saw the camera zoom in to a room window on a higher floor where the occupants had succeeded in breaking the glass. To our surprise, we saw that it was Master Charles in the room along with two members from the group. They started waving a white bed sheet to get somebody's attention in order to help them get out. But, you can imagine our shock when we heard an over-enthusiastic reporter babble in an excited voice that 'it seems the terrorists are surrendering as they're waving a white sheet!' What more proof that everything is always a matter of interpretation?

So much for the comfort of a suite in a five-star hotel overlooking the tranquil Arabian Sea. So much for the comfort zones in our lives. More often than not, events transpire that take us out of our comfort zones. In reality, it's not that we're taken out of our comfort zones but the fact that we are where we are – while the zone has changed its relationship to our existence.

I later asked Larry, who was trapped with his wife Bernie in their room, what went through his mind while all this was happening. This is what he wrote:

"... I was stricken with a deep and impactful fear. Upon realising that I could be facing death... there began a process of surrender. First, there was acceptance of the reality of the situation... knowing and fully understanding the gravity of the situation... the only option was to surrender to it. This came very naturally... not to avoid the prospect of losing one's life (by delving into the distractions of the mind)... in the complete understanding that this was what was happening and to try and avoid it by creating something other than the reality that was happening was useless."

What Larry meant was the surrender to 'what is' and not an imaginary 'what should be'. This acceptance of 'what is', is perhaps what made him come through with whatever equanimity was possible in such a situation. This is what made him go on to say, *"and in a strange way... I was honoured to have been able to participate in such a life-changing event... it catapulted my evolution in ways that only such a tragedy could."*

They were locked in their rooms in the middle of a five-star war zone and here we were sitting in the secure comfort of our home not even a block away, giving them live updates from the TV, of an event that they were a part of – here and now. Could it get more absurd than that?

"Life is stranger than fiction," Ramesh was fond of saying.

As events turned out, I wasn't able to thank Alan in person for his gift. It wasn't meant to be. In the months that followed, each time I lit an incense stick in front of my altar, I did so in the memory of Alan. I fondly remembered the little time that I shared with him and, in turn, was reminded of the fact of how we take the next breath of ours as well as our loved ones for granted while the incense stick of our lives gets consumed slowly, but steadily. One day, a few months later, I noticed that the incense stick in the holder had burnt only half way. Immediately, the thoughts came up: *Why did it extinguish midway? Did someone put it out? Was it a defective stick?* And then the thought arose: 'There goes the mind, searching for a cause-and-effect relationship'. It immediately reminded me of Alan, and how his life was cut short.

While we are conditioned to think that the sticks are supposed to burn right up till the end – sometimes God has other plans. That, strangely enough, reminds me of an anecdote that is but a grim pointer to what the truth really is.

The Life Insurance agent told his potential customer: "Don't let me frighten you into taking a decision. Sleep on it tonight, and if you wake up in the morning, let me know what you think."

Who faces a crisis?

We were up all night watching TV and giving updates to Master Charles on his mobile. The conversations had to be short because his phone's battery was running down. He also had to keep calling the mobile phones of other members of the group to keep them updated. Whenever we spoke to him, he sounded composed (to the extent one could possibly be in such a situation) even though, being the head of the group, he was walking on the razor's edge. He told us that there were six members of the group at the dinner table. What their fate was – he did not know. There were others who were dining at a separate table in the same restaurant and had left minutes before the terrorists arrived.

The phone in my room rang at 4.30 a.m. It was the Vice President of Synchronicity calling from Virginia, USA. She called to ask if we had any update on the six members, but I said we had none. She said that she had received a call from one of the members of the group, saying it was believed that Alan was at the dinner table and 'went down' with a bullet to the head. My heart sank. We had no news about Naomi. She said that it was believed the others were perhaps in a nearby hospital – one of them being Bombay Hospital. My family and I left immediately for Bombay Hospital. From here on, we were functioning literally like robots.

That's the thing about a crisis. In a way it brings you totally in line with what the moment has to offer. There is no time to think. Information is fed in and you react and respond to it. Ramesh referred to this as the 'working mind' as distinct from the 'thinking mind'. The working mind functions in the moment, while the thinking mind functions 'in the past', or 'illusory future'. The working mind deals with 'what is'; the thinking mind is more concerned with 'what should be'. In a crisis, the mind – the working mind – is totally engaged in the present.

It is only after the crisis is over that one wonders how one actually endured everything and saw the crisis through. The truth is that there was no 'you' in the crisis to see it through. There was just pure reaction and response happening, based on one's nature. Therefore, there is no 'me' that sees a crisis through, in the sense of a separate individual being involved in the crisis. The 'me' steps in later, and claims ownership of the response or reaction by saying – "'I' reacted this way." And this is when all the rationalising and conceptualising begins – "I should have done this instead of that. If only I had..." and so on and so forth *ad nauseum*, leading to blame, guilt, regret, condemnation, and everything else that goes with it.

If only we could live our lives 'in the moment' without a crisis dangling at the other end of the stick forcing us to. Having said that, the truth is that it is already so with each experience one has. When there is an experience, there is no 'experiencer'. It is the 'me' that steps in later and claims ownership over the experience – 'my' experience. Thus the experience gets established in retrospect as 'mine'. Such is the burden of identification with a separate name and form, a separate 'me' – a burden that is the mother lode of all experiences that 'I' am supposed to have had in the course of 'my life'.

On the subject of reaction and response, it is perhaps pertinent to point out a subtle difference. A reaction is, one could say, more unconscious. It is a knee-jerk reaction to what someone says or does. We react based on our past patterns and conditionings. The reaction comes out almost immediately, more so, when someone says something that we do not like.

When the identification with 'me and my story' is less strong, then what arises is a response. A response seems more measured as compared to a reaction, but the reason this is so is because the absence of reactivity makes it *appear* like that. When there is a lesser sense of individuality (me and my story), then one is open to 'what is'. If someone says something that one does not like, a response to the same will arise as the situation will be seen for what it is, 'whole'istically, and the appropriate response will be given, or rather, will arise. Some new age teachings point out how one should choose to respond and not react to a situation. This is quite hard for the 'me' to *do*, simply because it is the same 'me' that reacts that is now being told to 'respond'. This means, the 'me' has to be on guard before the next reaction comes up, and then when something is said or happens, it needs to watch out that it does not react but responds to the situation. This creates a sort of double-bind, with the 'me' having one more additional thing to *do* in order to respond and not react to a situation. Layer upon layer of 'doership' is laid on, as in a multi-tiered cake.

But when it is seen that everything is a happening that happens precisely because it is the will of God; when it is seen that everyone – like us – says things based on their patterns and conditionings; when it is seen that it is the same Consciousness that animates all of us, then the 'what is' is accepted for what it is (and not what it 'should be'), and a natural response arises. When this understanding goes deeper, it is seen that a happening is invariably met with a response and not a reaction. The 'me' needn't *do* anything in order to convert the reaction into a response. For, in doing so, it would turn the reaction into a re-reaction. That is why the wise always seem to respond to situations with equanimity. The fact is it is not a deliberate 'doing' on their part. It is simply what happens in their natural state.

Having said that, one cannot ignore the fact that some beings are prone to react in specific ways. In Vedic astrology, it is believed that even traits like anger are in the stars, and can be indicated in a horoscope. Ramesh used to say that in a man of understanding, anger is less likely to arise. However, when it does, as in the case of his guru Nisargadatta Maharaj, the anger will not be stretched in the duration of horizontal time. The next moment if someone were to say something funny, the sage would laugh. He would not stop himself from laughing because he had got angry with the person a minute ago. This is because a sage witnesses anger arise in a 'body-mind organism', which happens to be his in this case. The anger takes its course but the sage does not get *involved* in the anger. He is totally open to what arises in the next moment.

At the end of the day, whether it is a reaction or a response, there is no 'one' who reacts or responds to the situation. It is the 'me' that steps in later and claims that it reacted or responded.

In the name of God

The first thing we did was to check if we needed to visit the morgue at the Bombay Hospital. Mercifully, there appeared to be no cause for that. We were shown a list of those who were mortally wounded, but Alan and Naomi's names did not figure on it. If someone had told me the night before that, in a few hours, I would be doing the rounds of the hospital searching for those gunned down and possibly killed by terrorists in a fancy hotel in the neighbourhood, I would have scoffed at such a highly improbable scenario. But, as we all know, life can spring surprises.

We then decided to check on who else had been admitted. The first member of the Synchronicity group we found was Helen. She had been at the dinner table and had escaped with barely a scratch. This was in spite of the gunmen shooting low through the table-tops to get at those who were lying under them. Shortly after the initial burst of firing, a voice from the staff service area near the kitchen shouted, "If anyone can move, come this way!" That's when those still alive crawled to the door of the service area.

We were as thrilled to see her as she was to see us. It is amazing how a tragic event can bring one so close to someone one did not earlier know well enough. More often than not, it takes tragedies to bring people together. We become more loving, more vulnerable. Why? With a tragedy, we lose our sense of self in relation to something – that which we have lost. To compensate, we try to make up for this loss by deriving our sense of self from something or someone else.

When I was at a dinner with Eckhart Tolle in Pondicherry in 2002, I mentioned to him: "I just lost my grandmother. I sense a vacuum, a kind of hollow feeling – like a vacuum without (the physical absence) and a vacuum within. It is a sense of loss – something that was there and is no longer there now." When I lost Jeffrey, my lovable daschund, who had been with us for more than seventeen years, the same feeling had arisen. Looking at Eckhart,

I wondered aloud what it must be when one loses everyone or everything one loves at the same time, which would effectually mean that this vacuum would be all-pervasive: all around as well as within. He answered, "That is what enlightenment is." What he meant was the sense of self would no longer be derived from, and depend upon anything – especially something external.

At the same time, tragedies bring people together for a simple yet overlooked reason. We value 'our lives'. Not our individual lives – not 'my life' as opposed to 'your life' – but *our* lives. If you only valued your own life then there would be no need to reach out to others; where would the need be? What good is it to value your life if everyone else around you is dead? But just like when one falls in love one loses one's self in the other, similarly when we encounter a loss of any kind, our sense of self is diminished with that loss, and therefore, we find it easier to love others and reach out to them. As our sense of a separate self gets diminished, all that separates us also gets diminished. This is why we come together in the face of tragedies. Why do we have silent marches and come together for people who have died whom we don't even know? Because we value life. And that life is Consciousness.

Helen said that she was at the table and saw Alan take a bullet to his head. She thought that Naomi hadn't made it either. When Naomi saw that Alan had been hit, she leapt up to hug her father. Alan had seen the gunmen come in and had instructed everyone to get under the table, and to 'play dead'. Ironically, the bullet that hit him proved fatal. His daughter's instincts made her leap towards him and she was instantly taken down as well. It was perhaps Alan's quick response that helped save the lives of the other four at the table.

I told Helen that it was quite incredible that she escaped with hardly a scratch. She said it was perhaps due to the fact that she immediately started chanting *"Om Prabhu Shanti"* (a protective mantra that literally translates as 'Peace, Oh Lord!'). At first, I marvelled at her presence of mind in the face of rapid gunfire. Then, I thought that it was perhaps an 'absence of mind' that brought this mantra straight forth from her heart – after all, where was the time to think? But the irony of the situation was that in one instant, we had someone killing in the name of God, and in the other, we had someone chanting the name of God for protection. What a supreme drama being enacted by Consciousness, without which – in this living dream of life – none of what transpired could have taken place. Consciousness was the operating factor in both these individuals. If neither were conscious, neither could have taken God's name.

Which side of the door have you been placed on?

The four surviving members of the group at the dinner table had been taken to Bombay Hospital. They had been shot but were out of danger. But for the others stuck in the hotel, this drama played on for almost two full days. We knew that most of the group were staying put in their rooms and were safe for the moment, but anything could happen next. It is believed that the terrorists had even started going from door to door, in order to take hostages or kill more people. During the 26/11 trial, a security officer who helped the National Security Guard in their operation deposed before the court. He said that they had started to open the doors of the rooms on the 18th floor with a master key. They did not know which room the terrorists were holed up in, so it was a tedious task as they had to check each and every room, floor by floor. When they opened the door of room 1856, terrorist fire came their way. The commandos took shelter. One terrorist called out and said: *"Himmat hai to bahar aao, chhup chhup ke kyon maar rahe ho?"* (If you have the courage, come out of hiding and fight). To this, the NSG officer replied, *"Hum to bahar hi hai, tum andar ho!"* (It is we who are outside, you are the ones who are inside behind closed doors).*

Isn't life always a matter of perspective? Which side of the door of life are you standing on? Are you looking at the door opening or the door closing? Who's on the other side – a friend or a foe? One never knows, for sometimes friends become foes as well. But one thing is for sure; it is Consciousness operating through all those we consider either friends or foes.

The drama ends for some… and begins for others

Meanwhile, we saw on the TV how desperately the terrorists were trying to blow up the dome of the Taj Mahal Hotel, which was also under attack. It is a miracle how the dome withstood all that bombing. Fire and smoke billowed out from all sides and one would have thought it would collapse any moment. The visual of the dome collapsing would have been a symbolic visual victory, but it was denied to them. It was just not supposed to collapse in spite of all their efforts, in addition to the RDX that was put in to blow it up. Some things are just not meant to happen no matter what efforts we humans put in.

---

* *The Times of India, Mumbai Mirror*, Sept. 25, 2009.

During these two days, we took turns visiting the perimeter of The Oberoi Hotel. Of course, the hotel was cordoned off but one could still get pretty close to it. We were anxious to know if there was any news filtering out. I met some friends outside – college friends, health club friends, school friends. What an out-of-context social gathering this turned out to be! They had their loved ones dining at the hotel. They were all hopeful that everything was okay. It was then that I realised that perhaps there were very few who knew, at that time, the actual extent of the carnage inside. We did, for we knew there were six at the table and the four who escaped had seen what had taken place. Besides, we were in regular touch with those in the rooms. I said a silent prayer for them, but knew that the gravity of the situation did not offer much hope.

Finally, we got a call from Master Charles. He said it seemed that the danger was over, and the soldiers were going door-to-door, knocking on doors, and rescuing those inside. A bus was arranged to take the group to a hotel in central Mumbai.

We were shown a place to stand where we could meet the group as they walked out to the bus. But the next thing I knew, we had to defend our positions. The media was all over, lining up and ready to jostle for 'sound bytes'. In one such frenzy, I was jostled and found myself pushing back in the direction the push came from else I would be out of the designated area and standing with the commandos. The next thing I knew, a hand came out and clawed at my face. The lady from the media was angry as she had not succeeded in displacing me for 'pole position'. My sister Shibani told me that there was a cut on my cheek that had the hint of a bleed. In the diminished elbow room available, I pulled out my 'kerchief and dabbed randomly at my cheek. In the very next instant, a commando came over, took my 'kerchief, and gently started dabbing at my miniscule battle wound. It was cute and comical at the same time.

Because the crowds and media were all over the place, me and my sister were allowed to get inside the bus and wait for the group. We waited inside. They came and hurriedly got into the bus. As Master Charles got in, we hugged. No words were spoken. I sat by his side on the journey, holding his hand for a while. He said the hardest thing he had to do thus far in life was identify the bodies of Alan and Naomi on his way out from the hotel. It was a war zone; everything was gutted and burnt – the restaurant was a bloody mess.

All said and done, their ordeal was finally over.

For the others waiting outside, seeing that their loved ones were not coming out, yet another ordeal had just begun.

The happening

A movie multiplex is situated just across the road from The Oberoi. A few months after the incident, I went to see a movie there called *What Just Happened.* As I walked past the hotel, I thought to myself: *What an irony! Ramesh used to keep saying that everything is a happening. On 26.11.2008, there was a most tragic happening just across the road. Now, we were going to watch a Hollywood movie playing there called, What Just Happened.* Both were happenings, nonetheless. Everything just happens, and then we react to the happening... event after event, isn't life just a series of happenings? Some happenings bring pleasure and some bring pain. I remember, at one of Ramesh's talks, a visitor asked him, "But what is a happening?" I couldn't believe what I had just heard. He just could not follow what Ramesh meant when he said, "Everything is a happening." He asked Ramesh again, "What is a happening?" Ramesh, in all seriousness, replied, "A happening is something, which happens." I thought that reply took the cake. What a strange question, and the answer was even funnier. It only struck me later that perhaps the visitor was so identified with his reaction to events that he could not fathom that there was actually something that was 'a happening' to which 'he' was reacting. Could any other answer be given?

What registers in our consciousness – and gets deeply embedded – are happenings that give us maximum pleasure or maximum pain. The happening could be an event, or simply what someone says, or even a thought. Simple happenings like having a cup of tea do not have as much of an impact. Maximum pleasure makes the ego feel 'good', and maximum pain causes suffering and makes the ego feel 'bad'. The memory gets logged in our consciousness and then the ego craves for that which makes it feel good, and does its best to avoid that which makes it feel bad. Thus, there is a vested interest in the happening – the ego gets more and more involved and, therefore, entangled in this web that gets spun around itself, wanting some things to occur and others not to.

Meanwhile, the sage witnesses the happening as *a happening*, to which *a response* arises. He does not get involved in the response or, to put it more accurately, involvement in the response does not arise. The response is witnessed just as the happening is witnessed – without judgement. The sage would savour each sip from his tea cup for he is 'present' in the moment, while he is sipping his tea. He is not fastening seat belts on to his thoughts, or making roller coasters of unrestrained thinking go through his mind, to the extent that sipping the tea has become a secondary mechanical process and a mundane chore while his mind is surfing more important matters elsewhere.

The thoughts that arise as you read this are a happening. When the thoughts lead to thinking in the duration of time, that is the involvement of the ego in the thoughts. No wonder we say to someone, "What were you thinking?" We don't say, "What was your thought?" Throughout the course of our lives, one thought after another keeps popping up. Just like waves, thoughts arise, collapse, and then, new thoughts take shape. Like the phoenix, they take birth, get burnt to ashes when it is time, and new ones are born. But what would it take for all of our habitual thinking to be burnt in the fires of Awareness? The answer is clear: a happening!

The terrorist attacks brought collective grief to the citizens of Mumbai. The paradigm had shifted. To have terrorists from another country in your city undertake a shooting frenzy, and then have the drama go on for two days was something no one could have envisaged. Now, it has become a reality. This incident has been etched into the memory of its citizens and the scar will remain for a long time.

On the subject of movies, it's small wonder that everyone roots for the 'good' guys. It's not that those whom you consider 'bad' are rooting for the bad guys, while you and your gang of do-gooders are rooting for the good guys. Why? Simply because everyone thinks of themselves as the 'good guys', while the 'others' are the bad guys, the oppressors, the ones who have done wrong. Is it any wonder then that most movies have a happy ending, with the good guys winning battles against the bad? In *The Lord of the Rings*, the riders of Rohan are the universal good guys, the underdogs, outnumbered in their battle against the mighty Orc army of monstrous creatures. Who would want the bad guys in this case to win? And so what happens is that when the good guys win, we all win. Everyone is happy. Especially the producers of the movie when it scores at the box office!

The hotel reopens

Almost a year-and-a-half after the terrorist attack, The Oberoi reopened. It had to be completely renovated because of the devastation it had undergone. One Saturday, I was to meet my dear friend Xavier for lunch, and mentioned that it would perhaps be nice to eat at the newly reopened hotel. I thought of Alan and Naomi, and felt that it would be nice to eat in the same restaurant where they had their last meal – in their memory.

I wondered what emotions would arise when I entered the place. *Would there be sadness and grief? Would there be trepidation knowing so many had lost their lives in that space? What would the mood be?* As we walked in, I was pleasantly surprised to see that the entire floor of the lobby that used to be a pitch black was now stark white. It was a pure, spotless white that completely changed the atmosphere of the hotel interior. There was a blood-red grand piano right in the middle of the vast lobby; I thought the visual impact was quite symbolic – the music of life that was but a speck in the vast ocean of Consciousness. I am reminded of the words of Robert Frost: "In three words I can sum up everything I've learned about life: it goes on." Of course, he didn't mean his life; that was bound to come to an end sooner or later. He meant the One Life, and that life is Consciousness.

We entered the renovated restaurant and took a table on the side. We were initially silent. I could see the mind wander: *Where exactly did the terrorists approach from? Could they be seen through this window we were sitting against? Where exactly were Alan and the group sitting*? I could feel a tear welling up as the thought arose of Naomi leaping across to her father. The stream of thoughts was snapped when the waiter came with the menu. We placed our orders. I looked around. Everything appeared like it was business as usual. If the entire memory of what transpired was wiped out, one would not have a clue about what had happened here some time ago. 'What just happened' was relegated to history – it existed here and now only as a memory.

Our drinks arrived. We raised a toast to the memory of Alan and Naomi. A feeling of elation overcame me as I thought of them. A smile escaped my lips. Thoughts are a funny thing – one thought brings a tear, another, a smile. Next to us was a couple with two young children. The children, being children, were creating a ruckus while the parents were busy trying to calm them down. 'Life goes on' indeed. Events happen, forms disappear, new forms appear, but the One Life that is Consciousness goes on. The Phoenix – a symbol of immortality, of resurrection, of the end being the beginning – rises again and again, as it did that afternoon at 'Fenix'.

The new name of the restaurant couldn't have been more apt. To have spelt it 'Phoenix' might have been too obvious a reminder of the happening. This way, the phonetics were the same and yet, it was a silent tribute to the lives lost.

All in all, we had an enjoyable meal at Fenix. As we left the restaurant and walked across the lobby, past the red piano to the elevators, we could see the Arabian Sea in the distance through the large windows. Bright light streamed in, courtesy of the afternoon sun, and reflected off the stark white floor. I recently read an article on how scientists have invented a solar cell that destroys itself and reassembles perfectly. They were inspired by the plant kingdom. One problem with harvesting sunlight is that the sun's rays are destructive to many materials and they cause degradation of systems developed to harness it. But plants have a strategy to prevent this – they constantly break down their light capturing molecules and reassemble them from scratch so that the structures that capture the sun's energy are, in effect, always brand new. Meanwhile, the real reason I read the article was its caption, which caught my eye when I turned to the page. It said, in bold letters, Phoenix Power*. No wonder the legendary Phoenix does what it does. To harvest sunlight, to itself be an emanation of sunlight,

---

* *The Times of India, Mumbai Mirror*, Sept. 3, 2010.

it destroys itself and emerges anew, leaving the ashes of its former self at the Sun city. It has now been reborn to see the dawn of a new day. "The old order changeth, yielding place to new," wrote Tennyson in *The Passing of Arthur* – a retelling of the famous *Le Morte d'Arthur* by Thomas Malory.

We waited for the elevator. The red arrow down button lit up. We stepped in, the doors closed. The elevator headed to the lower lobby one level below. And the doors opened… to the next happening.

No question of forgiveness

An event like this almost always brings forth the issue of forgiveness. Can the terrorists be forgiven for this heinous act? Of course they cannot, but the reason is not what one thinks it is.

The world that we live in is one of duality with everything having its opposite – good and bad, male and female, beautiful and ugly, and so on. Duality is the framework of daily living. Duality is really not the problem, but *dualism* is. In daily living, we live as a 'me' separate from the 'other'. We treat the 'other' as an object and ourselves as the subject. What is overlooked is that fact that we in turn are the object of the 'other', who then acts as our subject. We usurp the subjectivity of the Source, God, and pronounce judgement after judgement on the object, based on what we consider right and wrong. And the 'other' does exactly the same thing. Rarely do we consider that we are instruments, through whom the same Source functions – the Source that is the Ultimate Subject. This is what is meant to be conveyed by the often-related analogy of the wave and the ocean in spiritual teachings. Each wave considers itself as separate from the other waves, forgetting that the content of all waves is water.

Therefore, when we forgive someone we act as if we are the Ultimate Subject – God, and bestow our forgiveness for the deed that has been done, whether or not the 'other' has asked for our forgiveness. Ramesh was not fond of the word forgiveness. He used to say, "If everything is a happening that had to happen according to the will of God, then who is to forgive whom and for what?" If we are all instruments through whom the same energy functions (in other words, we are all 'objects'), then how can one object forgive another object?

It is said that the first step of healing is to forgive others. Forgiving others is surely better than making one's body-mind a breeding ground for the scorpions of hatred, malice and resentment with which we end up stinging ourselves. One might say that it is better than not forgiving someone (not forgiving being at the bottom rung of the conceptual ladder of forgiveness). But, while one might say that one forgives somebody for what they have done, deep down does one actually feel so? How deep down does saying "I forgive…" really go?

What is then considered the next step in forgiveness is forgiving oneself for what one did, or felt, and so on. Or, we are sometimes told that we should first forgive ourselves and then, forgive others.

Could it be that the whole perspective on forgiveness is misconceived? Could it be that the only way to totally forgive someone is when the thought of forgiveness itself does not arise, not because one can't forgive the 'other', but… who is there to forgive?

When it is fully realised that nobody truly 'does' anything, but we are all instruments through whom the same energy functions, then where is the question of forgiveness? When there is total acceptance of what has happened, forgiveness becomes a non-issue. Total acceptance of what has happened is true forgiveness, with no 'one' to forgive another.

We may not like what has happened, and may take the actions we feel necessary in response, but we don't resist the happening itself simply because... it happened. Regarding the event, we cannot second-guess the will of the Creator when tragedies like this happen, just as we cannot know why God creates handicapped children. Ramesh would say, "What harm have they done and to whom? The only answer is that God created handicapped children because God created healthy children..."

A few days after the terrorist attacks, a friend mentioned to me that she felt like 'killing' the lone surviving terrorist. It goes without saying that it is a tempting thought. Though I am timid by nature and always tend not to engage in conflicts, I wondered if that is what I would do if I actually had a gun in my hand and the lone terrorist facing me. After one of Ramesh's talks, I went into his room and told him exactly this. I said, "I wonder what I would do in such a situation! I know what someone who has lost a loved one would most likely feel like doing, but I truly wonder what I would actually do – especially if the thought of the young thirteen-year-old girl being killed came to mind in that instant." He said, "That's precisely it – you have no idea what will happen – what the next moment will bring, what thought the next moment will bring. And even if you pull the trigger, then what is it? Anger in the moment – that's all. If the thought arose of all the innocent lives that had been lost in such a gruesome way, then that's just what might happen, even in someone who is timid by nature. But the honest truth is that one truly doesn't know what one would do in a given situation."

A few months before he passed away, Ramesh handed me some of his random jottings. One stuck in my memory, and it was on forgiveness. It said, "True forgiveness is forgiving yourself for wanting to forgive someone else for something he is supposed to have done." In other words, true forgiveness is the total acceptance of God's will. No question arises of a 'me' forgiving a 'you'.

This is perfectly reflected in what Jesus said. One of the first things Jesus is supposed to have said on the cross is, "Father, forgive them for they know not what they do." He did not say, "I forgive them, for they know not what they do." What humility, what compassion… to be cruelly and brutally nailed to a cross, yet have such words pouring forth!

Faith, Krishna and hope

It's around 8 p.m. on a weekday. I'm sitting on my bed with the TV switched on. A suicide bomber has blown himself up in Baghdad, taking seventeen people with him. Invariably, the news these days has the same flavour: someone else blowing themselves up in a mosque in Pakistan, Naxals ambushing and killing cops in India, something or the other happening in Kashmir, a bomb going off in Russia, a gunman going on a shooting spree in the USA… such an explosion of hatred everywhere. It's horrifying to see the grief, anguish, despair and shock on the faces of those who have lost a loved one in such a tragedy. The thought arose – there must be so many people by now who have lost a loved one in a terrorist attack, and the numbers must be climbing.

Only when a loved one has been killed in such a senseless way can one know what that pain really is. Yet for some viewing such images, empathy arises when these pictures flash across the screen. That's when 'their' pain is felt as 'your pain'. For others, it's just 'Breaking News' on the TV. Indeed, sympathy does arise – seeing these horrific acts makes one sympathise. But, sympathy operates in the domain of the dualism of the 'me' as separate from the 'other'. In other words, with sympathy, there is still a distance between 'me' and the 'other'. Empathy is when the veil of separation between 'me and the other' is thinner. It is a *felt* experience of oneness.

I read an account of a person who had lost his son in the terrorist attacks. He said, "Whatever little faith we had in God, we lost even that." That's the burden of the faith that we carry: faith that everything will work out for the best for 'me and my loved ones, and my life story'. When something disturbs that, or is not in accordance with what we think is in our best interest, we lose our faith in God. On the other hand, our life's experience is that everything does not go our way all the time. We've all faced challenges and difficulties that we'd rather not. Yet, we keep building expectations from God and negotiating with him through prayers, rituals and good deeds, so that all 'good' comes our way. And expectations lead to frustrations when they are not met. Could it be true faith if it is a faith that gets shaken because of all that goes wrong in our lives?

I lost my father when I was fourteen. Most certainly, I lost faith in God at the time and can therefore fully understand the emotion of 'losing faith in God'. But my life's experience in the years that followed taught me one thing: as long as the faith was dependent on something happening to 'me', it was a wavering faith. When something 'good' happened, faith increased; when something 'bad' happened, faith decreased. Where is the faith that would be unwavering, built on a solid foundation, built on a large immovable rock?

True faith in God is the faith of knowing with certainty that whatever happens is the will of God. Faith in God is the total acceptance that it is God's will that prevails at all times. Salvador Dali said, "And what is heaven? Where is it to be found? Heaven is to be found neither above nor below, neither to the right nor to the left, heaven is to be found in the centre of the bosom of the man who has faith."

Heaven is to be found in the heart of the man who has total faith that whatever happens is God's will: 'Thy will be done'. Then, tragedies like this don't get extended into tsunamis of hatred, condemnation, guilt, and so on, which tend to gnaw away at our insides over vast stretches of time, in addition to the grief in the moment that arises. All thoughts of *'Why me? Why did this have to happen to me? What did I do wrong? What did those who died do wrong?'* and so on and so forth don't arise when there is a total understanding that God's will prevails at all times. Then, one is totally there – totally present – with the grief when it arises. Full-on. In fact, there is only grief in the moment, without a 'me' getting involved in that grief and layering all sorts of conceptual thinking on top of it.

At a press conference, Master Charles was asked whether he felt guilty for leading the ill-fated trip that cost lives. Perhaps the questioner assumed that Master Charles, being a spiritual guide, was 'more informed' than others. Parts of his reply mirrored the highest teaching of Advaita. He said it would be as absurd to feel guilty about leading the pilgrimage, as it would be to judge the terrorists. "Our understanding of life is that reality is relative. There will be consistently the oscillation of relative polarities, whether you call them positive/negative, love/fear, subjective/objective… through oscillation of relative reality we evolve our balance and wholeness. All experience is valid and we can't really sit in judgement upon it and say this is right and that is wrong." And these are the words of someone who lost his right-hand man and his daughter in the incident.

Of course, this does not mean 'condoning' the terrorists. We will all respond exactly the way we think and feel we should. Apparently, some citizens who lost their loved ones have come together and sued governments; others have sued the hotels for lack of security; while, yet others have been overburdened with the grief and do not want to have anything more to do with the event, in any way. Master Charles was just giving a pointer to how his approach impacted one's individual suffering and subsequent attitude in relation to the traumatic event.

Over the last month, I saw two photographs in the newspapers that were quite moving. One was of a young Afghan boy, all of five years, with an AK56 gun in his hand and wearing what looked like camouflage gear, being trained for war. It was a shocking sight. The child was being conditioned from such an early age to play this role.

How would he distinguish between right and wrong when his whole worldview was being shaped like this by those around him in his formative years? More importantly, what must it take to give rise to such hatred that people think it is justified to train young children to take up arms?

The other picture I saw presented a completely opposite view point. It appeared on the day after *Janmashtami* – the festival celebrating the birth of Lord Krishna – a Hindu god. It showed a burqa clad Muslim woman walking on a street in Mumbai and holding her son, who was dressed up as the young boy-Krishna, in her arms. His skin was painted blue, he held a flute in his hand and had a peacock feather strapped around his head. The photo caption said that she was taking him to a school function on the occasion of Janmashtami. *'Why doesn't this image go around the globe?'* I wondered. Perhaps it's not sensational enough. I remembered what Eckhart Tolle said at his talk in Mumbai in 2002. He told the audience, "Spiritual gatherings like this don't make the news."

When I saw the picture of the Muslim mother with the boy Krishna in her arms, what arose was hope. Hope, which is different from expectation. It is perhaps a form of expectation, but it is expectation without the burden of wanting. When spiritual seekers would come to meet Ramesh, he would tell them not to despair. He would say, "When God has brought you this far, why should you think he will drop you here? Consider your glass half-full and not half-empty." That is hope. In this case, it is a hope for Peace, which perhaps is the most realistic of all hopes, simply because peace is our true nature. Why else would we fight for it? Take heart. In the words of

Nisargadatta Maharaj: "Insanity is universal. Sanity is rare. Yet there is hope, because the moment we perceive our insanity, we are on the way to sanity."

End Note:

Gautam's account of his experience of 26/11 shows the value of the non-dual perspective based on direct experience. His reflections demonstrate a holistic understanding of life.

A powerful example of how liberating this understanding is, is when he had lunch in the same restaurant where Alan, my husband, and my daughter Naomi had been killed by the terrorists. Every new moment brings the possibility of a new experience if we open to it. Gautam opened to the experience of the present moment, not the past moment that was gone forever. This is being fully human – to include all experiences in the continuum of life is to honour the sacredness of life.

His reflections in this essay inspired me to go to the Fenix restaurant on New Year's Day 2011 and sit at the same place where Alan and Naomi had sat for dinner that fateful night. What better way to honour the lives of my husband and daughter than to celebrate a new year by embracing a new moment that is fully alive in the here and now. As my spiritual teacher, Master Charles Cannon, said, "Death follows birth. Life is eternal." And so I broke through the barrier of the painful past memory to celebrate the eternality of life on the first day of 2011 – to invite new life into my life, to experience the love of Alan and Naomi that lives on in my heart, rather than their death in a time that is gone forever.

Kia Scherr
Mumbai, January 2011

NO GREATER LOVE

Your task is not to seek love, but merely to seek
and find all of the barriers within yourself
that you have built against it.

– Jalaluddin Rumi

"Love is wanting to do something for the other without the slightest expectation of anything in return." When I read this sentence in Ramesh's manuscript of *The Ultimate Understanding*, I felt it was not quite worthy of being included in it, simply because the book represented what Ramesh referred to as the pinnacle of his teaching of Advaita. One had read this sentence before and, while it was a truism, it didn't feel like a unique aspect of such a book.

It was only years later that I realised that it was not only profound but truly relevant to the book. The question that naturally arises after reading such a statement is: How is it possible for 'me' to want to do something for the 'other' without the slightest expectation? It is the nature of the 'me' to project into the future and 'expect'. How can the 'me' drop this expectation? It is not the 'me' that drops the expectation but, rather, the 'me' that gets dropped. And this can happen when there is the total annihilation of a 'me' as separate from the 'other'. When the self-identified 'me', identified with its actions, is annihilated, then there is no question of an expectation.

I have a friend who is now divorced. She mentioned that her marriage had been physically, verbally and emotionally abusive. Yet, she loved her husband to no end and, therefore, bore the abuse. She said hers, after all, was 'unconditional love'. I said that in no way was this love unconditional for there was obviously some condition being met, which made her constantly take the abuse. She did not take to this kindly, and said there was no greater love than what she felt and it was truly unconditional. Anyway, I kept quiet lest I lose a friend, but I thought I would run this conversation past someone I have known since childhood who is a therapist and specialises in relationship issues. My instincts were confirmed. The therapist outlined six scenarios of possible reasons why the wife took the abuse:

1) It was a compensation of some sort – 'I am inadequate in some way'.
2) It was need-based (any negative, repetitive behaviour is need-based).
3) It was because of some particular conditioning (e.g. being brought up to believe 'man is god' and can't do wrong).
4) It was a form of punishment because of some guilt she may have experienced (making up for the same).
5) If the relationship between the father and mother was an abusive one, the pattern could repeat.
6) It was a chemical reaction because some people are addicted to pain.

Whether it was just one or a combination of these reasons we were not in a position to assess, but what was clear was that the 'me' got something in return, and constantly expected something in return even though in this case it was suffering. Of course, the expectation was unconscious. Perhaps what would have been a better reflection of unconditional love would have been if she had walked away, so that the repetitive drama did not harmfully play out between the two individuals.

How can I learn to love unconditionally? I can't, simply because loving unconditionally is not something I can *do*. It is not something I as the 'me' can do, for unconditional love implies the non-existence of the 'me' as a separate entity. There is no 'one' as separate from the 'other' to *do* anything.

The term 'falling in love' is quite apt. What needs to be clearly seen is that it is the 'me' that literally 'falls' – in love. The separate 'me' falls away, which means that the love is always there – all it takes is for the 'me' to fall away for 'unconditional' love to shine forth. This is what happens when we fall in love. The separation is blown to smithereens; the walls of 'my' fortress are breached and come tumbling down like a ton of bricks. We are totally consumed by the 'other' simply because our 'me' is diminished, and all that matters is what makes the 'other' happy. But this does not last for long as the 'me' slowly creeps back in, thanks to its habitual conditioning of being a separate entity with a sense of 'doership'.

I remember an incident at one of Ramesh's talks. There used to be a row of three chairs facing Ramesh, on which visitors could sit and ask questions while all the others gathered around listening to the dialogue. A mike was clipped onto the shirt collar of the visitor who asked the questions, so it could be recorded. Once the person was done with his questions, he passed the mike to the person sitting next to him. That person politely declined as he didn't want to ask a question at that point of time. So, the first man went across to the third gentleman, clipped the mike to his t-shirt, and then went back to his chair. Witnessing this, Ramesh remarked, "This man has the understanding." What Ramesh was pointing to was that there was no need for this man to take the trouble, but what arose was spontaneous action in the moment as if he was putting the mike on his own t-shirt.

Does this mean one should go around affixing mikes on people's collars? Of course not – that would mean the 'me' deliberately 'doing' something in order to display an act of unconditional love. This would get the 'me' mired in more and more separation – precisely that which it was trying to avoid!

Ramesh was never fond of using the word 'love' in his satsangs. This was simply because the idea that people have of love is a personal love, even if they profess it is unconditional. Therefore, he would say, "I don't say that you have to love one another. All I say is don't hate one another. If all there is, is Consciousness and everything is God's will, then there is simply no 'other' to hate." In one talk, he went on to say that when there is no 'other' to hate then what it really means is that there is no 'other' (as separate from the 'me' to hate). When there is no 'other', then there is no 'me', and when there is no 'me', then *everything* is all there is. No wonder it is said that the primary *seva* (selfless service) is: do not harm another.

Maharaj said, "Live your life without hurting anybody. Harmlessness is a most powerful form of yoga... This is what I call *nisarga yoga*, the natural yoga. It is the art of living in peace and harmony, in friendliness and love. The fruit of it is happiness, uncaused and endless."

When there is no 'other' then true love is impersonal. When I mentioned this to a friend, he said that the word impersonal sounded too cold. I fully understood what he meant, as the word 'impersonal' carries with it a conditioning of something perceived as inhuman. But perceived by whom? Who else, but the 'me'? No wonder the 'me' perceives it as cold – simply because it does not involve the 'me' when it is impersonal. But what is truly meant by 'impersonal' is that there is no 'me' person as separate from the 'other' person. There is no separation. What could be more intimate than that? What could be more personal than impersonal love? What could be more intimate than there being no 'other' to be separate from?

Sages who advocate the path of *bhakti* (devotion) tell seekers to see God in everyone. What they mean is that the same energy – Consciousness – is functioning through all of us. It is simpler for some people to objectify this energy as a 'form' (let's say their guru or personal deity), and thus see God in everyone. Sathya Sai Baba refers to it as having an 'even vision'*, which is an appropriate term. Seeing with even vision means labels and judgements and all that the 'me' holds dear falls down like a house of cards, because it is not the separate 'me' that sees with even vision. Even vision is 'what is', without the barrier of separation propped up in front of it. However, it must be understood

* *Seeking Divinity*, Dr. John Hislop, Sri Sathya Sai Sadhana Trust.

that even when the barrier of separation is there, it is propped up on the impersonal ground of being, which remains forever unchanged. It remains what it was before the barrier of separation was put up and stays after it is brought down. This impersonal ground is simply the awareness – 'I am' (not 'I am Gautam' as a separate entity).

'Even vision' reminds me of an amusing anecdote Ramesh used to narrate in his satsangs. One evening he told his wife about how one of his clients had come over to the bank to discuss a 'personal' matter, which happened to be a huge argument with his wife. He kept going on and on about how his wife was in the wrong, and Ramesh replied, "You are right." However, the next day Ramesh was surprised that the wife had dropped by at the bank. She met Ramesh and kept going on and on about how her husband did this and that, said this and that, and so on. Ramesh kept replying, "You are right." At this point, Ramesh's wife Sharda told Ramesh, "But how could you have told both of them that they were right?" Ramesh looked at her and said, "You are right."

The explosion of love took place with the Big Bang when Consciousness stirred and the manifested universe came into being and brought with it duality – male and female, good and bad, beautiful and ugly, 'me' and the 'other' and so on. But the 'me' got mired in *dualism*, considering itself separate from the 'other', and pronouncing judgement upon judgement on the 'other', usurping the subjectivity of the Source – the One True Subject, without realising that it is itself an object, just like the 'other', when viewed through the eyes of the 'other'. This 'me' thinks it is falling in love when, in effect, what is happening is that it itself falls into the ocean of love that already exists as 'us'. The little 'me' tries hard to love, and lights the fires of love on that which already is its foundation – Consciousness – the reason for its existence in the first place. The 'me' cannot love someone unconditionally because it itself builds up barriers to unconditional love – that is the Consciousness that binds everyone together. The 'me' claiming to love unconditionally is like an arsonist claiming he lit the fire that made the volcano erupt. This is what made Rumi state: "Your task is not to seek love, but merely to seek and find all of the barriers within yourself that you have built against it."

I remember when I was with a friend in London and we were browsing some stores in Covent Garden. She was beautiful and radiant, and men were constantly trying to strike up a conversation with her. We entered an antique shop near the Watkins bookstore and almost immediately the shop owner looked at her and said, "Hellloooo… where are you from?" She promptly replied, "Yesterday." He was a bit flustered and was searching for a reply, and something to move the conversation forward, but it wasn't meant to be. I was impressed by her spontaneously witty, yet true reply… for aren't we all yesterday's people carrying with us our baggage of resentment, greed, envy and malice; what should have been, what should not have been, and so on and so forth; living in the past and projecting into the future; doing whatever we can to escape from the present moment – 'what is'?

The 'me' is notorious for being preoccupied with itself – *How will this help 'me'? How will this improve 'me'? How will this fulfil 'me'?* This spotlight on 'me' takes one further away from the other person. This self-obsession causes loneliness. But when it is truly seen that there is no 'other' and we are all instruments through whom the same energy functions, then loneliness disappears just like a shadow does when one steps out into the noonday sun. Then the 'me' is no longer lonely but is *alone*, for there is no 'other'. An incident at one of Ramesh's talks clearly demonstrates this point.

There was a lady in her late fifties who mentioned to Ramesh that she felt lonely as her husband had left her, the children had grown up and lived far away and, now that she was past her prime, people didn't stop to look at her on the streets like they used to. She was feeling miserably lonely and did not know what to do. Ramesh's reply was immediate. He told her (to paraphrase): 'It's simple – find others who are lonely and then go and spend time with them. Go to an orphanage – where there are children with no parents to love them – and spend time with them. That way, you won't be lonely and neither will they'. Almost all the eyes in the room were moist. What would happen as a natural outcome of this is that the obsession with 'me' being lonely would stop and the focus would shift to the 'other', to someone who perhaps needed it more – in this case, orphaned children. *No separation. No loneliness.*

To the 'me', bringing down the walls of its fortress of separation seems like a Herculean effort. Of course it is. This is because the nature of the 'me', mired in *dualism*, is one of separation. The 'me' did not create itself, the ego, in the first place. The Source created the ego. Nothing need be done by any 'one', as we all already exist as That. Nothing need be done to bring down the walls. Could it get any simpler? When it is clearly seen that there is no 'other' to hate, when it is clearly seen that there are no walls to be brought down, simply because none existed in the first place, then it is realised that there is another world, but it is this One.

"Life is love and love is life. What keeps the body together but love? What is desire but love of the self? What is fear but the urge to protect? And what is knowledge but the love of truth? The means and forms may be wrong, but the motive behind is always love – love of the me and the mine. The me and the mine may be small, or may explode and embrace the universe, but love remains."

– Sri Nisargadatta Maharaj

ACKNOWLEDGEMENTS

My grateful thanks go out to:

My mother Santosh, always the first one to go through my writings. Her sensitive feedback is invaluable.

Master Charles Cannon, whom it has been a privilege to meet and interact with.

My sisters Shibani and Nikki, who are always there for me.

Shiv Sharma, for his editorial inputs. He is one of the best editors a publisher could hope for.

Satish Gupta, one of India's finest spiritual artists, for the Zen drawings that you find in this book.

Gary Roba, a wonderful friend, with whom working together is like playing a jugalbandi. We have closely worked together on some of Ramesh's books as well. His quest for perfection is unending. It reminds me at times of what Ramesh once told me, "Gautam, you're such a perfectionist!" "Hardly," I replied, "as compared to you."

When Ramesh had given me his copy of a book by Wei Wu Wei, I was astonished to see how he had underlined some sentences in different colours – red, green, black... and there was a colour code in the margin indicating what each colour stood for. Then, there were other sentences that were double-underlined! All I used to do was use a six-inch scale and a pencil to underline what impacted me. I asked Ramesh, "Sometimes, I wonder what's the point of being a perfectionist when 99 per cent of the people wouldn't even notice it." He retorted, "It's for the one per cent!"

Chaitanya Balsekar, for his encouragement after reading the initial essays. Ma Amodini Saraswati, Nan Umrigar, Linda Ragsdale, Kia Scherr, Mary Cox, Meena Kapur, Rohit Arya, Neela Bahl and Roger Castillo for their inputs on different essays.

Xerxes Baria and Priya Mehta, for their inputs on the cover design.

Vilas Naik, for the photograph on the back cover.

S. K. Mullarpattan, for regaling me with anecdotes about Maharaj.

Gabriel Halfon and Dr. Shirish Bhagwat, who unknowingly contributed timely material.

Roselyn D'Mello, Sunita Kripalani, Smriti Chawla and Pooja Singhal, for assisting with the proof reading.

Girish Jathar and Sanjay Malandkar, my trusted colleagues, for the layout and DTP.

TITLES OF GAUTAM SACHDEVA PUBLISHED BY YOGI IMPRESSIONS

Pointers from Ramesh Balsekar (2008)

The Buddha's Sword (2009)

For information on Gautam Sachdeva, visit:
www.gautamsachdeva.com

The author may be contacted on email:
mails@gautamsachdeva.com

For further details, contact:
Yogi Impressions Books Pvt. Ltd.
1711, Centre 1, World Trade Centre,
Cuffe Parade, Mumbai 400 005, India.

Fill in the Mailing List form on our website and receive, via email, information on books, authors, events and more.
Visit: www.yogiimpressions.com

Telephone: (022) 61541500, 61541541
Fax: (022) 61541542
E-mail: yogi@yogiimpressions.com

Join us on Facebook:
www.facebook.com/yogiimpressions

Follow us on Twitter:
www.twitter.com/yogiimpressions

ALSO PUBLISHED BY YOGI IMPRESSIONS